MEG SANGSTER

THE MARY RAINE STORY

FROM PUTNEY TO PERTH

ISBN 0 646 49925 4

Published by Meg Sangster

Publication sponsored by The Raine Medical Research Foundation

Cover photograph of the Wentworth Hotel courtesy of *The West Australian*

©Cover designed by Jane Clarke of Zigzag Graphics

Printed by Success Print
7a Goongarrie Street
Bayswater
Western Australia 6053

For my children

Mark, Joel, Julienne

CONTENTS

Author's note		iii
Acknowledgments		v
Preface		vii
Chapter 1.	Here's one you won't have to keep	1
Chapter 2.	We have come to God's own country	19
Chapter 3.	Always be in debt: It is the only way to make money	29
Chapter 4.	Speculate to accumulate	49
Chapter 5.	It is my melancholy duty	69
Chapter 6.	'Rainee'	85
Chapter 7.	We were two pals	00
Chapter 8.	It's the best room in the hotel	123
Chapter 9.	We hope you'll say 'Yes'	137
Chapter 10.	We want to retire	151
Chapter 11.	So dearly loved: So sadly missed	161
Chapter 12.	The long day closes	171
Chapter 13.	The Raine Foundation: A unique achievement	185
Interviews conducted by the author and written submissions		195
Archival and general sources of reference		196
Reference origins - books, articles and reports		197
Notes		199
Picture credits		203
Index		204

AUTHOR'S NOTE

This book is not an 'official' biography of Mary Raine. I have interpreted her life and built her story from the limited information available about a woman who, though a public figure, was essentially a very private person.

My building blocks have come from many and varied sources, but I hesitate to claim that no material has been missed. Perhaps my writing will encourage others to fill any remaining gaps in Mary Raine's history.

Because I enjoyed a close business and personal relationship with my subject during the final twelve years of her life, I have drawn extensively on my own observations and experiences.

To that extent, The Mary Raine Story is also a personal memoir of the years I shared with her and is, I hope, a tribute to a very special woman.

Note: Australia adopted its Decimal Currency System in 1966.

£1.0.0 Australian became $2.00 though the relative value has changed over the years.

ACKNOWLEDGMENTS

It is now more than one hundred and twenty years since Mary Raine's birth, and forty years since her death. When I decided that her story should be told, I knew it would not be easy to access much of the information I needed.

Nevertheless, because of the exceptional co-operation I have received from a number of sources, this book reveals many interesting and possibly unknown facts about my subject.

Important contributions have come from second and third generation family members, friends and staff, who shared personal experiences and recollections. Their names are listed under the section titled Interviews Conducted by the Author. I wish to say a heartfelt thankyou to each and every one.

I warmly acknowledge the outstanding help I have received from the custodians of the various libraries and archives I have used. Their patience and genuine interest has been beyond expectations. These institutions are listed under Archival and General Sources.

Special appreciation is due to Lyn Ellis, Executive Officer of the Raine Foundation, who compiled the final chapter of the book, and has taken a personal interest in my research.

My thanks also, to Jane Clarke for her kindness in designing the cover and to Lyn Ellis, Ilse Erber and Jo Donnellan for careful proofreading.

I thank West Australian Newspapers for the use of copyright photographs and The Raine Foundation, Guildford Grammar School and Broome Historical Society for the use of archival material.

My children have encouraged me to follow the advice I have always given them and finish what I had started. I thank them for their loving support. Joel, who came to the rescue when my limited computer skills found me out, deserves special mention.

Most importantly, my heartfelt thanks to Sally Clarke, who encouraged me on every step of the way.

Finally, I thank The Raine Foundation most sincerely for its support in sponsoring the publication of The Mary Raine Story.

PREFACE

Her customers called her Ma. Perth people referred to her as Ma Thomas, but from the time our paths crossed in 1948 I knew her as Mrs Raine, the name she acquired on her marriage to her beloved Joe in 1943. With the passage of time since her death in 1960, my heart and mind have come to remember her as Mary.

When I met Mary she was about seventy years of age. Very tall, somewhat gaunt, and bean-thin, with the slight stoop often seen in people who are taller than those around them. She wore her hair short and slightly waved. No doubt the hairdresser's art was responsible for its unusual corn colour which was maintained consistently. Her creamy English complexion was almost transparent and, even at that stage of her life, there remained traces of a former fragile beauty. During the day she would wear a long skirt and blouse with a cardigan drooping from her thin shoulders. In the evening this combination was replaced by a simple dress - silk in summer, velvet in winter. An enduring favourite was a long purple velvet dress which defied the vagaries of fashion and I very much doubt that she ever discarded it.

Born Mary Bertha Carter in Putney, London, in 1877, she was the eldest of twelve children, ten of whom survived. As was not unusual in those times, her school days ended when she was fourteen and she went from being a pupil to being a teacher's assistant. She saved assiduously from her meagre earnings and in 1900, with just £100 in her pocket, she sailed for Australia on the steamship *Jumna.*

A series of adventures and misadventures brought Mary to Perth, where, in 1904, then aged twenty-seven, she met Bill Thomas. Although she strongly disapproved of his drinking habits, she finally succumbed to his determined courtship. It was not a happy union. She found it ironic that he was thrown from his horse and killed on one of the rare occasions when he was sober.

After Bill's death, Mary threw herself into the business of acquiring hotels and other properties, showing an acumen that was rarely seen in a woman in those early years of the century. She was an entrepreneur when few would have known the meaning of the word, much less been able to spell it! In an era when most women accepted a secondary role to men, she forged a business empire through sheer determination, hard work and calculated risk-taking, single-mindedly pursuing her goals. Her flagship was the Wentworth Hotel.

Mary was the least pretentious person I have ever known. A hands-on publican - the term used to describe a hotelkeeper in those days - she worked tirelessly every day of her life, driving her frail frame when others were wilting, all for the satisfaction of doing the job well and doing it successfully. 'I lose sight of the money. It means nothing,' she told me often. Frugal habits, born of necessity in the early years, stayed with her throughout her life. Even when she was, arguably, the wealthiest woman in Perth, she lived as simply as she had when every shilling counted.

On 3 December 1943, Mary married Arnold Yeldham Raine, a popular farmer from Manmanning, who over the years had been a regular guest at the Wentworth. He was known to everyone as Joe, but Mary seldom called him other than 'Rainee'. Although Joe was thirteen years her junior, the marriage was a success. He was a loyal and devoted pal - her description - and Mary told me on many occasions that her years of marriage to him were the happiest of her life.

Sadly, Joe suffered a severe stroke in September 1956 and died from its aftermath in February 1957. His death left Mary bereft and inconsolable. She had never foreseen the possibility that she could outlive him and was in no way prepared to deal with this devastating loss. She was convinced that Joe could have been saved had medical expertise in the treatment of stroke and heart disease been more advanced. This conviction was the driving force in her decision to leave the bulk of her estate to the University of Western Australia for the establishment of a Medical Research Foundation. Thus was born The Raine Foundation. Comprising property valued at £1,000,000 at the time of her death in 1960, her estate was one of the largest private bequests ever made to an Australian University.

Mary abhorred ostentation and discouraged any form of public recognition of her generosity. It was her wish that 'the net income from the bequest be applied by the University in and towards seeking, diagnosing and investigating the nature origin and cause of diseases in human beings, with initial emphasis on arteriosclerosis and allied diseases, and the prevention, cure, alleviation and combating of such diseases.'

There are few, if any, embellishments in this account of Mary Raine's life. I have relied mainly on what she told me herself during the twelve-year period when I shared a close business and personal relationship with her and her husband. Prior to her death, she started a journal describing her early years in Putney, London, and recounting the series of events that caused her to leave her home and sail to Australia. It is unfortunate the journal did not progress beyond that point, but the information was invaluable in accurately recording Mary's early life - the trials, successes, failures - and exploring the forces that shaped the strong, focused woman she became.

In my writing I have endeavoured to do justice to an exceptional woman, whose legacy has already benefited, and will continue to benefit, all West Australians, also to bring to light a forgotten part of this State's colourful history.

I hope this book will play some part in ensuring that Mary Raine's name is never forgotten.

Her monument is, and will continue to be, the positive results achieved through medical research made possible by her bequest. I know she would be well pleased.

Chapter 1

Here's one you won't have to keep

1877 - 1900

Caught in a brisk spring breeze, the blue cotton pinafores hardly kept pace with flying black boots and swinging gold plaits.

'Come on Daisy. We'll miss the show if you don't hurry.'

'Wait for me Birdie. You run too fast. Anyway, we're going to be in awful trouble when Father knows we've been to see the bridge opened.'

'Do stop fussing and hurry. You'll never do anything interesting if you always wait for someone to tell you it's all right to do it.'

The young girls joined hands to make a final dash towards the beckoning gaiety of the park ahead. On a high rotunda in its centre a band played exhilarating marching music, as well-dressed ladies and gentlemen strolled and chatted in small groups, whilst keeping an eye on the ornate gates through which the carriage bearing the Prince and Princess of Wales would soon arrive.

The year was 1886 and the Royal couple was coming to officially open the new Putney Bridge, a graceful stone structure of five arches, connecting Fulham, on the Middlesex bank of the Thames, with Putney on the Surrey side. Putney - not far from the heart of London. Catch the south-western-bound train at Waterloo, pass Nine Elms and Clapham Station and you're there.

Mary Bertha Carter was born in Putney, England, on the 17 February 1877. She was the eldest of what would grow to be a family of ten surviving offspring. Because she carried the same given names as her mother, to avoid confusion she was always called 'Birdie' within the family circle.[1]

Towards the end of the nineteenth century, Putney was a mix of working and lower middle class families. Times were difficult for those at the bottom of the social ladder. For the Carter family, the arrival of a new baby every two years, or even less, meant that the challenge to put food on the table kept father, Charles Henry Carter, depressed and preoccupied.

Charles had married Mary Bertha Appleyard in 1875. It had been such an unlikely union that he pondered repeatedly on how it possibly came to pass that he, Charles Carter, with no sign of a secure future, or indeed, prospects of any kind, had been accepted by one of the Appleyard girls. There was money in that family, and Mary had been expected to marry into a family of equal wealth.[2] The fact that they met in the first place had been highly unlikely, given the difference in their backgrounds. However, the families shared an interest in music and came together from time to time at local concerts and entertainments. What started as rather awkward recognition gradually developed into a comfortable friendship and eventually Charles plucked up courage to ask Mary if he could call at her home.

Mary was a strikingly pretty girl. An abundance of wavy brown hair framed classic features and her smile was warm and generous. When they first met, her air of quiet confidence made Charles a little uneasy but he could not deny the attraction. When Mary Appleyard accepted his nervous marriage proposal, he faced the daunting prospect of formally asking her father for her hand. Her parents were appalled that she was prepared to marry beneath her social standing. However, Mary was determined and, in spite of her parents' opposition, the marriage went ahead. She had not chosen wisely. In future years she discovered, as many young women do, that love is not only blind, but also financially inept.

The wealth she had turned her back on became a Holy Grail for her eldest daughter, and the Mary Bertha of the next generation became consumed by her determination that one day she would be 'as rich as the Appleyards'.[3]

Soon after young Mary's seventh birthday the family, then comprising three girls and one boy, moved from their address in Putney to a larger house in Waterloo Road.[4] At that time Putney was a working class district. It is interesting that over the years the suburb has become increasingly fashionable, due no doubt to its proximity to the business heart of London. Today Putney would present an image far removed from that of the late 1880s.

When seven years old, Mary showed spirit and determination unusual in a girl so young. She was tall for her age, slight and wiry. Her fair hair, hung in plaits, framed a strong face dominated by searching blue-grey eyes. Being the first born of a growing family she learned early to take responsibility for her younger siblings, and always seemed older than her years.

Moving house caused a flurry of anticipation. The family had been assured that the new home was 'much bigger' and that conjured up all sorts of possibilities. When moving day arrived, the furniture was loaded onto a horsedrawn dray. Bundles of household crockery, pots and pans, clothing and other possessions were placed carefully to protect chairs and tables. Their parents constantly warned the children to check that everything had been gathered up and nothing left behind in forgotten corners.

The real excitement came when unpacking started at the new address in Waterloo Street. Mary noted, with disappointment, that it was not so very much bigger than the home they had left. At least there were more bedrooms and she and Daisy, the second-born in the Carter family, had been promised that they would have a room to themselves.[5]

A heavy rather forbidding doorway opened to a bare-boarded entrance. When the furniture had been put in place, the home was typical of thousands of others of that era. To the left of the entrance was the perfect spot for the tall mirrored hallstand, with its row of brass coat hooks and partitioned sections to accommodate dripping umbrellas. The drawing room on the right set the tone of desired respectability, with an overlarge settee and two matching chairs covering most of the tired carpet square. Crocheted antimacassars on backs and arms did not quite disguise signs of wear on the tapestry covering, but the welcoming depths of the seats gave an illusion of comfort. The sideboard displayed photographs and items of bric-a-brac so popular in Victorian England. The next door off the central hallway led to the dining room. It was spartan and functional, accommodating a solid rectangular table surrounded by high-backed wooden chairs, leaving room only for a large floor-to-ceiling dresser displaying plates of varying sizes, cups, saucers, serving dishes and jugs. Beyond these two rooms the aspect became progressively humbler. The bedrooms were furnished with bare necessities, there was a very large kitchen, and the laundry was housed in a small shed behind the house, next to a tiny patch of earth where Mary's mother planned to grow vegetables.

Mary started her education at a government school in Rupall Street, about a quarter of a mile from the new address. She was a good student, and whilst still quite young, displayed qualities of leadership and organising skills. After school each day Mary revelled in her self-styled role as 'King of the Kids', devising games in the street and around the Putney railway station to keep everyone occupied until it was too dark to play. Her favourite game was to pretend she was the teacher. Seating her playmates on the flight of steps behind the station, she would deliver her own 'lessons' and reward the best pupils with sweets bought with the one penny allowed by her mother.[6]

Even this one penny would have been hard to spare had young Mary's grandmother Appleyard not paid the family a small allowance during her lifetime. It was an effort to make things a little easier for her daughter.[7] She also persuaded her husband to make a will leaving his estate to be equally divided between his sons and daughters. This was a departure from the usual in those days, when sons only were recipients of family inheritance. Young Mary's grandfather acceded to his wife's wishes, but years later, in a fit of pique after a family disagreement, he changed the will and left the entire estate to his sons. When near death he regretted this and expressed the wish to again change the will to include his daughters. Sadly, he did not live to implement the alteration and on his death the entire estate went to his sons; another cruel blow for young Mary's mother and her family.[8]

The struggle to make ends meet was inexorable. Charles had acquired a fruit and vegetable stall under Waterloo Bridge. At least it provided cheap produce for his own table, but business was far from good. He worked long hours with little reward. Mary was about nine years old when she began helping at the stall. She would take over whilst her father went home for tea or an evening meal. She did not see this as being a chore, but actually enjoyed the task, and became very adept at coaxing customers to purchase something extra.[9]

Mary was expected to take care of her brothers and sisters, share with her mother the burden of running the house and help her father in providing for them all. A staunch ally in the cycle of duties was her sister, Daisy, who was less than two years younger than Mary. The two forged a close bond that remained throughout their lives. Both were very musical, a talent their mother recognised and encouraged. There was no money for a piano, but she smothered her pride and asked, indeed pleaded with her eldest brother, to buy one for her girls.[10] To his credit, he did so. She taught them herself and encouraged both to sing and to dance.

It was midway through Victoria's reign. London was home to two and a quarter million people, their numbers being continually boosted by a steady stream of eager immigrants. After all, outside of China and India, London had been the largest centre of population in the world for hundreds of years. Indeed, the more fortunate and affluent Londoners considered their city to be the centre of the universe. The rewards of prosperity, though, had not filtered down to the residents of Putney where the average yearly income was £120.

Mary was not yet ten years old when the unemployment crisis of 1885-1886 hit London. Hundreds of jobless men marched in Pall Mall and Trafalgar Square. Baton charges by police failed to keep angry marchers from the Square and the demonstration culminated in 'Bloody Sunday', 13 November 1887.

Two years later, Londoners faced the even more spectacular dock strike, when rioting workers demanded a minimum wage of sixpence per hour. The catchcry was 'a fair day's pay for a fair day's work'. These events made a lasting impression on the young Mary. She learned the value of money and the value of working time. When she became an employer herself, she earned the reputation for being a very fair boss, but she also insisted that the reverse of the catchcry was adhered to. 'A fair day's work for a fair day's pay'.

Whilst unemployment and poverty gripped the richest nation in the world, London prepared to celebrate Queen Victoria's Golden Jubilee. This lavish event also made a lasting impression on Mary. In her brief journal she recalled the excited build-up to that historic day in June 1887.

> New statues of the Queen seemed to emerge every day, showing her in every conceivable posture, and at every stage of her life: either stout as she was in old age or slender as she was when a girl.[11]

Souvenirs which ran the gamut of taste from elegant to tacky, appeared in hundreds of shop windows. Every possible variety of plate, cup, mug and jug, was offered alongside automatic bustles that played 'God Save the Queen' whenever the wearer sat down, teapots representing Victoria's head with the lid a crown, and walking sticks with her head the knob. One which could be considered reasonably elegant was chosen by the Prince of Wales as a gift for his mother. It was an inkstand. The lid was a royal crown which lifted to reveal the Queen's face reflected in a pool of ink. She was said to be very taken with the trinket.

On that special Monday, 20 June 1887, Mary, then aged ten, stood with thousands of excited schoolchildren watching the Queen accept the adulation of her subjects. Sixty years later, Mary described the scene as the monarch passed by.

> She drove in an open landau, drawn by six cream horses with colourful Indian cavalry forming the escort. She wore a black bonnet decorated with diamente and white lace, and matching

black silk lace-trimmed dress. She kept nodding her head to one side and then the other; she was just like an automaton. She didn't smile; she just nodded her head.[12]

Every school child, Mary among them, received a china mug featuring the monarch's profile, and a commemorative scroll.

In a childhood where special occasions were few and far between, Mary's father offered a rare treat when he took her to the exhibition mounted as part of the Jubilee celebrations. The highlight of the day was to ride - at the cost of one hard-earned shilling - on one of the new-fangled horseless carriages on display. The experience made a lasting impression on the girl from Putney. Much later in her life she recalled the wonder of it and the excitement of sitting up there on something that moved along without horses, whilst a man walked in front waving a red flag.[13]

Mary referred to the Locomotive, or Red Flag Act passed by Parliament in 1865. This limited the speed of 'road locomotives' to two miles per hour in towns, and four miles per hour on the open highway, with an attendant walking sixty yards ahead, carrying a red flag by day and a red lantern at night. Wealthy automotive pioneers lobbied to repeal the Act in 1896, successfully claiming that the Act was holding back the industry's development. By 1890, light steam vehicles were capable of being driven at fifteen miles per hour for long distances over British roads.

With the passage of time, more babies were born to Charles and Mary Carter. Unfortunately, business at the fruit and vegetable stall did not provide for the growing number of mouths to be fed. Young Mary, now twelve years old, was expected to spend every moment away from school caring for her younger siblings, or working at the stall. It became her responsibility to go to Covent Garden markets to buy for the business. She was paid one penny for this chore and always, without exception, she spent it on something to eat.[14] Each day brought evidence that times were getting harder, money was becoming scarcer and she started to worry about her future.

The Appleyard family had diverse business interests, among them a number of shops providing fresh fish and poultry. After

Charles Carter's brothers-in-law inherited the family wealth, there had been a suggestion that Charles should take over one of these shops; perhaps this was seen as a way of helping their sister's family enjoy a better standard of living. At the time, Charles allowed pride to rule his head and dismissed the offer out of hand. However, he now had to accept that proceeds from the fruit and vegetable business could no longer keep his growing family. Reluctantly he agreed to accept the offer and was relieved to discover that there was a more consistent demand for fish and poultry from a shop than for fruit and vegetables from a stall under a bridge.[15]

Charles liked to spend his evenings at the local inn playing billiards. He expected Mary to join her mother in keeping the shop open until midnight. Mary records that she didn't mind doing this and, once more, made a game of coaxing customers to buy more than they had come in for. The worst part was returning home to face the task of fixing the old-fashioned shutters in place for the night. Even between them, Mary and her mother could not lift their weight; it was then up to young Mary to find a kindly constable to give them a hand - something she was always able to do.[16]

Around the time of her fourteenth birthday Mary fell ill with a very bad attack of German measles. She was surprised when her father visited her room. He was not normally given to any degree of closeness with his family. In her journal Mary recalled the occasion.

> I remember my father coming into my bedroom, sitting beside my bed and asking me very seriously how I intended to earn my living. I was still far from well and his words came as such a shock that I felt I had no right to eat until I got a job.[17]

What to do? It was midway through the school year but Mary had taken her father's question so much to heart that she determined to find some kind of work without delay. As soon as she was well enough, she lodged an application with the School Board to become a probationary teacher and was accepted on the understanding that eventual employment would depend on her success in the qualifying exam at the end of the year. With only six months to study the full year curriculum, and although her tutor did his best, Mary failed the examination. The tutor, a Mr Christian, was aware she was not well. Now, witnessing her distress at failing, he offered her special tuition. After just three months, Mary tackled the exam again and was accepted as a probationary teacher.[18]

A huge weight lifted from her shoulders. At least she was now on her way towards a career. A requirement of the course was that she teach for twelve months before taking the first-year examination. She was posted to a school in a very poor part of London. Mary recorded that the children were dirty and ragged. She found her job difficult and depressing and was having second thoughts about her choice of career, when she was pleasantly surprised to find herself transferred to the Galley Wall Road Board School, near the London docks. This school was as poor as the one she had left, but she noticed that the atmosphere was happier, even though the headmistress was a very sick woman who could not tolerate the least noise. Because of this the children and their teachers were very quiet and discipline was exceptionally good.[19]

Mary was extremely happy in her work at the school and was bitterly disappointed when changes at home disrupted this pleasant situation.

Charles Carter had the opportunity to buy a small tobacco shop in North London. Business at the fish and poultry shop was reasonably good and it would mean another change of address, but here was an opportunity to free himself of obligation to the Appleyards. For this reason he was relieved to take the plunge and again try something new. He realised that young Mary was not happy about leaving the Galley Wall school, but he refused to let that consideration influence his decision. Mary was heavy-hearted when the time came to tender her resignation. She was still only sixteen but she left with a reference that suggests an unusual degree of maturity. The head teacher who wrote it could never have guessed how prophetic her words would prove to be. 'I am of the opinion that Mary Carter will be very successful.'

Galley Wall Road Board School
Girls Department
Bermondsey.
May 17th 1893

Gentlemen,
Mary Carter has been a pupil teacher on probation for nearly six months in the above school.
She is obliged to leave owing to her home being too far from school. She has given great satisfaction during her probation in this school. I find her willing, punctual and industrious. Her discipline is very good for so young a teacher and I am of the opinion that she will be very successful. We regret very much that she has to leave.

I am

Yours obediently

J.C.Green (Head Teacher)[20]

Mary successfully applied to be transferred to a school quite close to the new address. Unfortunately, the school had never had a probationary teacher and, more importantly, the head mistress didn't want one. From the very first day she made poor Mary's life a misery. Nothing was right, nothing pleased her. Try as she might, Mary found it impossible to get any kind of approval for her efforts. A failed singing lesson closed one door and opened another. As Mary records:

> I remember I was told to give a singing lesson to a very unruly first standard. I sounded the tuning fork and took the lower C, but not one child was able to sing such a low note, and the lesson was one more disaster. It had a good result however. I found I had a very deep contralto voice, but it needed a lot of training. The singing lesson was a turning point in my life.[21]

Mary knew she was at the crossroads. It was one thing to decide that teaching was not for her, but another thing entirely to decide what her next move should be. Much as she hated the new school she couldn't even think of leaving until she had something definite to go on to. Mary dreamed of having a job that she really loved. She envied everyone she saw going about their work - train drivers, shop assistants, even hawkers with their flowers or pots and pans. Never one to burn her bridges before she was certain that the next step would move her forward, Mary persevered at the school, but also worked at her father's tobacco shop in her free time. With the extra money she was earning, she started taking singing lessons.[22]

The move to North London signalled a change in the Carter family's fortunes. The tobacco shop prospered and, encouraged by its success, Charles acquired a second small shop in the same area. He asked Mary to take over its management. She happily accepted her father's offer and immediately tendered her resignation to the School Board.

Mary had become an eye-catching young woman. At seventeen, she was almost six feet tall, but carried her height with elegance and poise. A photograph taken at this age captured the essence of her spirit - feisty, confident, ready to take on the world. The fragile beauty of her face seemed almost at odds with the determined set of her shoulders. As a legacy from the need to grow up in a hurry and her early training as a school teacher, she was at ease when meeting new people and facing new situations, and was never at a loss for the right word.

Mary's singing voice showed enormous promise. Her teacher encouraged her to perform at local concerts to gain experience and confidence. She enjoyed this new episode in her life and harboured a dream that it might be possible to pursue a career on the stage. Quite soon an opportunity did present itself. An uncle, her father's brother, married an actress. By mere chance, during a visit to the Carter home, she heard Mary practicing and was impressed by the quality of her voice.

'Why don't you apply for the chorus in the opera and panto? I could give you an introduction to Sir Augustus Harris.'[23]

It was an exciting offer and Mary acted on it immediately. On the day of the audition, though in a frenzy of nerves she steeled herself to produce a good performance and landed a three-year contract to perform in opera and pantomime. Mary recorded the milestone in her journal. 'My salary was by no means princely and averaged, with matinees, about £2.0.0 per week, but at least I had a job I loved, and was earning my own living.'[24]

The first season was a great success and Mary felt very secure with two more years of her contract to run. Then fate stepped in. Sir Augustus went for a holiday to Folkestone, where he caught a chill which quickly developed into pneumonia. He was dead within a few days. All existing contracts were cancelled, his theatres were taken over, and for Mary, the round of job applications had to start all over again.[25]

She decided to concentrate on opera and an audition was arranged with a German Impresario named 'Gran'.

> 'I was very ambitious.' Mary recalled. 'I chose as my solo the aria and recitative from Nachesda. Unfortunately, without a piano, I went slightly flat in the recitative. I should have chosen something better known and easier to sing. I failed the audition but was asked to apply again later on. This I did, and was accepted for the season.'[26]

It was a busy time in Mary's life and a happier time than she could ever remember. Additions to the Carter family had continued to arrive every two years, but at least the income to support them was now more assured. Mary was holding down three jobs. Every morning she worked on her father's accounts, then rushed off to the matinee performance at Drury Lane. She fitted in a stint at the tobacco shop before returning to the theatre for the evening show.[27]

At about this time, Mary had her first serious romance. The young man was an engineer, the son of a judge and from a highly respected family. However, he was a Roman Catholic and Mary was Anglican. At the turn of the century, religious prejudice was firmly entrenched in all levels of English society. It was accepted that the romance would not progress to marriage and in due course the young couple drifted apart.[28] The scenario was repeated when Mary met, and fell in love with, a tall good looking Irishman who had trained for the priesthood then given it up and taken a job as a London postman. He suggested that Mary consider changing her Anglican religion. She was not prepared to do this.[29]

The contract with Drury Lane had been for one season only and with the final performances approaching, Mary auditioned for

Courtesy The Raine Foundation

Mary Bertha Carter - aged about 17

work at the Adelphi Theatre. If successful she would have evening shows only and no matinees. She had not felt really well for quite some time and hoped that a lighter workload might help to speed up her recovery. However the work at the Adelphi was spasmodic and despite a nagging awareness that she was still not well, Mary again signed on for the Christmas season at Drury Lane.

When she fell off the stool in her father's office, her mother sent for a doctor immediately. He diagnosed typhoid fever and ordered Mary's urgent admission to hospital, where she remained for three months. At that time little was known about the treatment of typhoid and Mary was put on a starvation diet that took her to death's door. She survived. However, she lost her contract, her luxurious blonde hair fell out, and worst of all, she lost her singing voice. When she was well enough to return to the stage she found that her beautiful voice had all but gone. She could not sustain a single note.[30] Fortunately, some measure of her talent returned after her convalescence, but a singing career was no longer an option.

In 1897, when Mary was twenty, London was, once again, gripped by the excitement of a milestone in the reign of Britain's longest serving monarch - Queen Victoria's Diamond Jubilee. Giving the event a name had required lengthy deliberation, there being nothing in existing protocol to cover such a celebration. Though industrial unrest and unemployment continued to plague the country, when 22 June arrived there was no visible shadow to mar the occasion.

The special day was decreed a public holiday. Wooden stands were erected along the route the Queen's entourage would take to and from St Paul's Cathedral; Whitehall, the National Gallery, Charing Cross Station and St Martin-in-the-Fields. Since crowds had swarmed into London from the country and from abroad to see the new young Queen crowned sixty years earlier, the city's population had tripled to nearly four million. Undeterred by dull grey skies, thousands were already on the streets by seven in the morning. Troops in scarlet uniforms and bearskins lifted the atmosphere and the spirits of the onlookers, as did the activities of peddlers hawking souvenir Jubilee pennants, flags, programs, balloons and mugs. When Victoria's State landau finally appeared it was greeted with veneration as well as enthusiasm, and many of the onlookers wept openly, overwhelmed by the emotion of the occasion. Remembering the event years later, Mary said that her lasting impression was of a very old lady performing the ritual required of her without quite being a part of it. The Queen's own recollections of the day were considerably more exhilarating. In a reference from her published letters and journals she remembered the occasion.

> Queen Victoria in her Letters and Journals
> John Murray (publishers) Ltd.
> Dense crowds between Paddington Station and Buckingham Palace gave me a most enthusiastic reception. It was like a triumphal entry. The windows, the roofs of the houses, were one mass of beaming faces, and the cheers never ceased. On entering the park, through the Marble Arch, the crowd was even greater, carriages were drawn up amongst the people on foot, even on the pretty little lodges well-dressed people were perched. Hyde Park Corner and Constitution Hill were densely crowded. All vied with one another to give me a heartfelt, loyal and affectionate welcome. I was deeply touched and gratified.[31]

The bout of typhoid fever meant that Mary had lost everything she had worked for. All the rosy dreams of success on the stage had become just that - dreams. Her mother urged her to take a longer convalescence, but Mary knew her father expected her to start paying her own way again. She braced herself for the soul-destroying task of finding employment, but it did not prove to be as difficult as she had feared. She was accepted as an invoice clerk with a men and boys' outfitters called 'The Scotch House', and Mary's duties included relieving counter staff for lunchtime breaks.[32]

As with everything she ever undertook, she threw herself into the new job with zest and enthusiasm. In no time at all she convinced her employer that he would make more sales if he displayed the merchandise better.[33]

'Put things where customers can see and touch them,' she said.

Following the tradition of the time, the shop was arranged with counters along three walls making a U-shape facing the entry doorway. The stock was housed in boxes, piled one upon the other behind the counters. Mary suggested small display islands be placed in the empty centre of the store, so that a variety of goods would catch the attention of customers, who may have come to buy something quite different. Swayed by Mary's optimism her boss implemented the changes and was pleasantly surprised when sales figures increased dramatically.[34]

Mary was very much in tune with the changing business scene in the inner-city area. About this time a Yorkshireman named William Whiteley had established himself as 'The Universal Provider'. He owned stores throughout London, revelling in his claim that there was nothing on earth he could not supply, a boast he made good. Apprentices at his stores were trained in a new approach to selling. Some years later, Richard Burbidge, a former head of Whiteley's provision department, transformed Harrods from a one-man grocery shop into a store with an annual turnover of £250,000 - a fortune in those days. Today, Harrods is a retailing institution.

Mary, together with John Breckenridge, ran the Scotch House office. John, the correspondence clerk, was a bit of a dreamer, always entertaining Mary with his grand plan to emigrate to Australia as soon as he had saved the fare to make his escape.

'There is nothing here for the likes of us,' he would say to her. 'Do you know that in Australia you can get a grant of land if you are prepared to work on it? You can get nothing here. There's gold in Australia. People are making fortunes every day in places called Kalgoorlie and Coolgardie. That's where I'll be heading as soon as I get there.'[35]

True to his promise, John did set sail for his Eldorado. Their paths never crossed again, but what he had said to Mary remained in the back of her mind. When John left, the boss decided that the jobs of invoice clerk and correspondence clerk could be combined and he offered the new position to Mary. It carried an increase in salary and she accepted immediately.[36]

Meanwhile events in South Africa saw Britain facing the threat of war. On 10 October 1899, an ultimatum drafted by Jan Smuts and signed by F W Reitz, State Secretary for the Transvaal, was delivered to the British Parliament. It reminded Britain of the terms of the London Convention in respect to Uitlanders, demanding that she withdraw her troops from the border, remove from South Africa all troops that had arrived since 1 June and recall troops now on their way to South Africa. Britain was given until five o'clock on the afternoon of Wednesday 11 October 1899, to accept these terms, or the Transvaal would consider the British to have declared war.

The demand was not acceded to and, on 11 October 1899, war began in South Africa between Britain and the South African Republic.

It had been patently clear that war was inevitable, but Britain was not prepared and there was a serious shortage of men and supplies. The first of these problems was solved by a surprising rush of volunteers from Britain and from the colonies. London was gripped with tense excitement. The British actually seemed eager for war.

Even so, scarcely anyone believed that the war would place a serious strain on Britain's resources or that it would last more than a few months. Wildly cheering crowds turned out to farewell volunteers, among them the famous City of London Imperial Volunteers.

There were many such departures and, sadly, many lists reporting the names of loved ones killed, missing or wounded in action. The sieges of Kimberley, Ladysmith and Mafeking were avidly followed whilst they were in progress, and wildly celebrated when they were relieved. In her journal Mary recalled that 'excitement was intense'. In reality, the country quickly grew tired of war.

At The Scotch House, as elsewhere in the city, business was depressed and, now that the reality of war was hitting home, London was steeped in gloom. Early excitement evaporated quickly, giving way to highly vocal criticism of the Government for allowing the country to become embroiled in a war over matters that should have been settled around a conference table.

Mary began to wonder if things would ever get back to normal. Certainly, she did not intend to spend the rest of her life managing a menswear store. She had to move on. But where could she go?

John Breckenridge's enthusiasm for Australia kept niggling at the back of Mary's mind. Perhaps he was right and there was no future in this country. How often had he declared, 'If you're not born a toff, you'll spend your whole life at the bottom of the heap.'

Shortage of money was a continuing source of friction in the Carter household. One evening, when father Charles had stayed rather later than usual at the local ale-house, he returned in one of his bouts of morbid self-pity. Standing at the head of the table he surveyed his offspring without much affection. 'I've got six daughters here to keep, and I suppose I'll be keeping them for the rest of my life.' Mary sprang to her feet and proclaimed defiantly, 'Here's one you won't have to keep.'[37]

The very next day she booked her passage to Australia and persuaded Daisy to go with her. The year was 1900. In Mary's purse was her life's savings of £100.[38]

In the years following the turn of the century, the fortunes of the Carter family improved significantly. It is interesting to note that grandchildren who were not around to observe the initial struggles, recall their grandparents' home as comfortable and relatively affluent. Mary Coward and Beryl Hobson, daughters of Mary's sister Laura (Lolly) Cooke, remembered only those later years and were surprised to read of the early privation and hardship Mary described in her journal.[39]

Once her decision was made Mary never wavered. However, the realisation that she was leaving her much-loved mother was unbearably painful. They had always been close and had shared many trials in the early years of Mary's life. When they said goodbye she had no way of knowing that she would never see her mother again.

Chapter 2

We have come to God's own country

1900-1902

In March 1900, Mary and Daisy said goodbye to all they had known and boarded the steamship *Jumna* bound for Brisbane, Australia. One of the first steel-hulled steamers, a 4,844 ton vessel, 410 feet long and 48 feet wide the *Jumna* had been built for the British India Line in 1886. She carried the name of an earlier vessel, a sailing ship lost in February 1882 off the coast of southern Western Australia en route for Hobart. The new *Jumna* was one of the early recipients of quadruple expansion machinery, a feature confined to the bigger, faster steamers, because the larger engine rooms required meant a loss of freight-earning space. Accommodation was for 207 First and 76 Second Class, steerage, passengers.

Mary and Daisy travelled steerage. The cabin accommodation, shared with eight other young women, was basic, even spartan, but no less comfortable than their cramped room in North London. Not fitted with a bilge-keel to minimise rolling, which became standard for steamers built just a short time later, the *Jumna* lurched and heaved alarmingly. The English coastline had scarcely faded from view when the girls realised that seasickness would be more of a problem on this voyage than lack of creature comforts.

With the gruellingly monotonous journey lasting almost ten weeks, the girls determined not to surrender to the inertia that came with having so little to do. They made a conscious effort to take an interest in what went on around them. The day usually started about 6.00 a.m. On Thursdays, luggage 'wanted on the voyage' was brought up and placed on a designated area of the deck. It was diverting to watch people going through their trunks, getting out what was wanted, locking away what had been discarded. A couple of stowaways were apprehended hiding among the luggage and the poor frightened youths were unceremoniously trundled up on deck by the scruff of their necks. It was not unusual to find young men taking their chances in this way. Surprisingly, they were not punished, but were set to work shovelling coal. Probably punishment enough!

As the ship approached Port Said the heat became unbearable and it was impossible to sleep. Passengers were encouraged to take bunks up on deck - ladies on one side of the ship and gentlemen on the other. It was important to rise early and move everything back to the cabin before sailors started washing down the decks, or there'd be a wet awakening.

By welcome contrast to the heat, there were long pleasant days when the ship glided gracefully through the gentle blueness, and time could be passed watching flying fish and schools of porpoises playing close by. More difficult were those days when the seas raged and swelled and the girls succumbed, along with most of the passengers, to the miseries of seasickness. Daisy was severely affected. Mary discovered that she could fight the nausea by lying down. Port calls for re-coaling were eagerly anticipated but did little to alleviate the enervating boredom and sameness of each day.

As the time for arrival drew near, Mary started to experience a kind of numbing dread. What did the future hold for them? If Daisy had any misgivings, she kept them to herself. Such was her confidence in Mary that she never considered for one moment that her older sister might not be able to cope in the new country, or in the city of Brisbane where they were to disembark.

In the year 1900, Brisbane was a city of close to 120,000 people. From the time of its earliest settlement, Queensland attracted immigrants, mainly from the United Kingdom, in larger numbers than any other Australian State. In 1891 the State was the preferred destination for newcomers to Australia and, at that time, only forty-five per cent of the population was Queensland-born. Unfortunately, economic problems, caused by a depression and a series of natural disasters, caused the government of the day to halt its immigration program midway through the decade. It was 1898 before there was sufficient confidence for the scheme of assisted migration to be reintroduced, and Mary and Daisy had availed themselves of this when deciding on Brisbane as the port of entry into their new country.[1]

Years later Mary recalled the trepidation and anxiety she felt on leaving the now familiar deck of the *Jumna* and taking her first step onto Australian soil - or rather, the drab, forbidding planks of Brisbane's wharf. She glanced at Daisy, standing silently in her shadow. They must have presented a forlorn picture, looking rather the worse for ten weeks at sea and guarding the battered trunks that contained all their worldly possessions. A kindly Providence must have been watching. A middle-aged woman had been eying them since they disembarked, and they were surprised to see her approaching. 'Are you girls expecting to be met?' she asked.

'Well, no,' Mary replied, and went on to explain their situation. The upshot of the meeting was that their new friend offered accommodation in her home until such time as they were able to find work. The offer was a godsend and they gratefully accepted.[2]

The first consideration for Mary and Daisy was to find a job quickly. They lost no time in venturing out to try their luck, and soon discovered that if they wanted to start earning without delay they would have to accept bar work. A query about theatre work, or clerical work, or shop work, was invariably met with the same response. 'No. There's work for barmaids. Start right now. Take it or leave it.' They took it.[3]

As the sisters were to learn, hotel work led them into a new world. At times, a rough world. The hours were long and the work was not easy.

In Brisbane at that time, hotels opened from 6.00 a.m. to 11.00 p.m. Monday to Saturday. These trading hours were the most generous of any of the Australian States. Mary and Daisy enjoyed the day shifts best, when the bars were relatively quiet. The rush was on around 6.00 p.m. when workers knocked off, and it was hard to keep the drinks up to the mass of clamouring customers. About 9.00 p.m. free sandwiches were put out on all the bars and this brought a fresh influx of drinkers. Saturday, being pay-day, saw the heaviest drinking. With beer selling at sixpence (5 cents) a bottle or fourpence (3 cents) a pint, it was possible for the average man to get drunk for 25 pence (20 cents). Consequently, drunks were a very common sight on the streets.

Mary and Daisy could not even count on having Sundays off. This was the only free day of the week for most workers and, despite the efforts of the churches and temperance societies, illegal Sunday trading was commonplace. There was pressure on the government to legalise the practice, but rather than alter the legislation the Commissioner of Police was instructed to relax its enforcement. At the time when the girls were working in Brisbane, all but two of the city's hotels opened on Sundays and were as busy as on any other day of the week.

Mary and Daisy started work at the National Hotel. Necessity is a great teacher and both girls were quick to learn. They soon became adept and popular barmaids. However, the National was in the least appealing part of town and when they were offered work at the Phillips, a newer hotel situated in the main street of the city, they were pleased to move on.[4]

The long rest imposed by the sea voyage had resulted in Mary recovering her singing voice. Her new employer, after hearing her perform, encouraged her to use this talent as an added attraction at his hotel. Her renditions of popular songs attracted extra custom and she enjoyed a small measure of fame as 'The Singing Barmaid'. Her performance came to the attention of a man called Percy St John, who produced a show in Brisbane called the Opera Comique Theatre. He offered Mary work in the local production, as well as an opportunity to go on tour with the company. She was wildly excited at the prospect of returning to the theatre. Sadly, after just one week as a performer, her voice deserted her again, this time, in the worst possible way. She was on stage, the orchestra was playing, the conductor signalling her to commence, but the sound would not come! The audience and the management were not amused and, for the second time, Mary's singing career came to an abrupt end.[5]

Undaunted by this setback, Mary decided it was time to look further afield. She and Daisy were now experienced barmaids and, from reports they had heard, there was always bar work to be found in Sydney. Why not try their luck? The precious £100 she had left home with was still intact and, buoyed by the assurance that they were by no means destitute, the girls said goodbye to Brisbane and headed south.

The Sydney that Mary and Daisy travelled to in 1901 was a booming metropolis. Although the city had existed in Melbourne's shadow until the 1880s, it survived the depression of the 1890s and had made rapid progress by the turn of the century. Located as it was on the shores of a spectacularly beautiful harbour, much of its development emanated from the wharves, docks and warehouses at the northern end. The Rocks, to the west of the city, was a port slum which attracted the criminal element to its many taverns, whilst the high land to the east of Woolloomooloo and Surry Hills was home to the mansions of the wealthy.

After the gold rushes, Sydney's population grew from 96,000 in 1861 to almost a million in 1901. The city centre became the commercial core, surrounded by workers' cottages and factories, with a growing system of tramways, ferries and railways fanning out to the residential suburbs of the skilled workers and the middle class.

The train journey was tedious and uncomfortable but when Mary and Daisy stepped out at Central Station, they were immediately caught up in the general feeling of optimism. Their success in finding jobs as barmaids simply by presenting themselves at a likely looking hotel, prompted them to write home with understandable excitement. 'We have come to God's own country.'[6]

The girls might well have settled in Sydney had Mary not been offered the management of a country hotel in New South Wales. It seemed an opportunity too good to refuse and was certainly a step in the right direction. However, the offer did not include Daisy, and Mary was reluctant to leave her. It was decided that Mary would accept the job and arrange for Daisy to join her when she was more certain what authority went with the 'management'.

Mary found herself on a train heading for Nyngan. Back in 1902, Nyngan would have been little more than a dot on the map. Situated on the Bogan river in the Western district, it is some two hundred kilometres south east of Bourke. Mary travelled on the train with another Mary, who had accepted the position of cook. For both girls the first look at their new place of employment was a bitter disappointment. The hotel was broken down and neglected - more like an abandoned building than a business premises. Like most country hotels of the time it was not particularly large - almost a shell, containing bars fronting both sides of its corner position. A balcony teetered precariously over the rough footpath, barely supported by its straining uprights. Smudged and grimy windows in surrounds of flaking paint, provided less than adequate light to negotiate the dark narrow stairway leading up to equally dark narrow rooms. All in all, it was a less than welcoming first glimpse for the new staff. But worse was to come. The place appeared to be totally deserted.

The two Marys resisted a strong temptation to head back to the railway station. Instead, they knocked on doors until a slurred voice demanded to know who was there. When the owner, their prospective employer, finally emerged, their worst fears were realised. She had obviously been drinking but made no apology for her condition. Instead, she launched into a tirade of abuse against the world in general and her own lot in particular. Most of what she said meant nothing to the girls until it finally became apparent that the hotel had no guests, no customers, no stock, and the brewery and wine merchants had refused to deliver supplies until outstanding bills were paid. The girls had to decide whether to beat a retreat or mount a rescue operation.[7]

With the lapse of one hundred years, I have been unable to establish with certainty which of Nyngan's early hotels was the scene of Mary's challenge. I am indebted to Nancy Brooksby, secretary of the Nyngan and District Historical Society, and to the town's centennial publication 'Nyngan on the Bogan', for some facts that suggest strongly that the present Nyngan Hotel was the site of the saga. It was built in 1883 and named the Commercial, but more popularly referred to as the Nyngan. It is the oldest hotel in the town, situated on the corner of Dandaloo and Nymagee Streets and has enjoyed major alterations and upgrading over the years. The present owners have reconditioned the hotel in conformity with its original architecture and it is now officially named the Nyngan Hotel.

Mary Raine always enjoyed telling the story of how she saved the Nyngan Hotel - or rather Pub, as she always called it. I heard it many times over the years.

There was no suggestion that her cherished £100 would be put at risk, but Mary did have a plan. In short, the two Marys each contributed £1.10.0 from their meagre funds. With this total of £3.0.0 they went down the road to the rival hotel and bought bottles of beer, wine and spirits - returned to the derelict hotel and sold their purchases over the bar at 'glass' prices. This effectively doubled the value of their investment. Now with £6.0.0 to spend they repeated the visit to the rival hotel. That sum of money bought a lot of bottles in those days, and Mary always laughed as she recalled that the opposition publican even organised delivery for them. The upshot of the rescue operation was that the hotel eventually became viable and even flourished. It became both popular and prosperous as Mary entered into the social life of the small town.[8]

The success did not go unnoticed by the liquor merchants, and in due course the hotel was put back on a regular trading basis. Only one in a million could possibly have pulled it off, but then, Mary Carter was one in a million.

Even though the bar trade had been restored and guests returned to bedrooms and dining room, forces beyond Mary's control meant that her success was difficult to maintain. She had been at the hotel for about eighteen months when New South Wales was gripped in a devastating drought. Nyngan was in the heart of the worst affected area and the result was crushing for the small town. The Bogan river, lifeblood of the district, dried to a few muddy pools. Parched animals gathered, jostling to find the few remaining trickles of liquid life, whilst wild goats stripped bark from the trees in a vain effort to slake their thirst. Sheep and cattle sagged and dropped in their tracks. The hopelessness was tangible. In despair, farmers were salvaging what could be carried and walking off their properties whilst cursing cruel fate and cloudless skies. Against all odds, Mary rode out the storm.[9]

From the time of her arrival at the hotel Mary had been concerned at the cruel treatment her employer's de facto husband meted out to his young son. The situation eventually became so bad that she felt compelled to report the matter to the police. The upshot was that the child was removed to a safe home, the man was run out of town, and the employer again consoled herself by getting blind drunk every day. Eventually, she simply took off.

Mary had been the licensee of the hotel in all but name since her arrival in Nyngan two years previously, and the representative of Resch's Brewery, the owner of the property, lost no time in asking her to take over the hotel. Mary was delighted. It seemed too good to be true. It was. The liquor licensing laws of the time did not permit an unmarried woman to hold a hotel licence.[10]

Thoroughly disheartened to find that hard work had not finally paid off with the final reward of her own hotel, Mary returned to Sydney, where Daisy had continued to work as a barmaid. The sisters decided to go back to England. It was a difficult decision, especially for Mary. The fact of returning meant she had failed, when prospects in this country seemed so promising. After a good deal of agonising, they bought tickets for the return journey on a German ship. The voyage home would take them through the Great Australian Bight, with a brief stopover in Fremantle before heading westward.

The Bight lived up to its reputation, having scant regard for the comfort of travellers braving its turbulent waters. Huge waves crashed upon the ship's decks as it tossed like a cork for days on end. Daisy was so seasick that Mary called the ship's doctor for help. He was strongly of the opinion that it would be unwise for the girl to continue the voyage. There was little sense in ignoring his advice and the two left the ship at Fremantle, planning to continue the trip home when Daisy had recovered.[11]

Chapter 3

Always be in debt. It is the only way to make money.

1902 - 1924

The ship that carried Mary and Daisy to Fremantle was among the first to test its new harbour facilities. Using plans prepared by C Y O'Connor, work to upgrade the harbour had begun in 1892 and was only completed early in the 1900s.

In the 1850s the P & O shipping company considered Fremantle harbour unsafe for its vessels and refused to allow mail-carrying ships to call there. Other shipping companies were encouraged to do likewise and make Albany, with its safe anchorage, the main port of call. This left Fremantle a secondary port, necessitating the development of a mail and freight service overland between Perth and Albany. The P & O company resisted all overtures from the colonists to alter this decision, and the directors were adamant that until Fremantle was made safe for its shipping, they would continue to use Albany.

Had the ship berthed at Albany it is quite possible that Mary and Daisy would not have disembarked. Her experience in Nyngan had convinced Mary that country towns were not for her.

The voyage from Sydney had been a nightmare. The prospect of continuing on to London didn't bear thinking about. Mary and Daisy were almost relieved to act on the doctor's advice and leave the ship when it berthed at Fremantle.[1] They had been due to arrive at about 6.00 a.m. but the difficult crossing had slowed the ship's progress and the estimated time of arrival was now 10.00 a.m. Well before that time, the girls joined excited groups of passengers leaning over the port rail waiting for their first glimpse of land. There was a buzz of anticipation when the outlines of small islands became visible, the coastline emerging as a thin black line edging a carpet of grey mist.

Most on board were bound for London and the ship would be in the port of Fremantle for just two hours. Few of the passengers were disembarking or even going ashore, and when Mary and Daisy stepped onto the unwelcoming wharf, clutching the travel bags containing all they owned in the world, they felt very alone. A friendly shipping office clerk pointed them in the right direction to catch a train to Perth. 'The station is only about two hundred yards from the wharf, and you'll be there inside forty minutes.' They set off defiantly to see what fate had to offer at this new destination.

It was mid afternoon. Others might have considered it a priority to find somewhere to stay. Mary had other plans. Find hotel work and the problem of accommodation would be solved. They made a tour of the city block and were impressed by the number of hotels. Taking their courage in both hands they presented themselves at the Metropole Hotel, choosing it because it was larger and more imposing than others in the area, and therefore more likely to be in need of staff.[2] It was situated in Hay Street, obviously the heart of the city, a triple-storey brick building with a very elaborate facade. Mary noted with a pang of nostalgia that it adjoined the Theatre Royal.

The girls had made a good choice. The Metropole had been built as recently as 1894 for Thomas George Anstruther Molloy and offered luxuries previously unheard of in Perth: One hundred bedrooms with up-to-the-minute furnishings, six saloon bars, and two spacious billiard rooms, just to name a few of its attractions. The three-storey building, incorporating the hotel and the Theatre Royal, is today protected under Western Australia's State heritage laws. The integrity of the original remains, though the street frontage has been converted into shops surrounding an arcade now known as St Martins.

By an amazing stroke of good fortune, temporary bar work with live-in accommodation was available for Mary and Daisy. They were elated. This was an auspicious start to what was planned to be a brief stopover until Daisy was strong enough to continue the voyage to London. The wife of the hotel proprietor was very kind to the girls and took them under her wing. When their temporary jobs were coming to an end, she found work for them at another city hotel.[3]

Their new jobs were at the Central, not far from the Metropole, situated on the corner of Forrest Place and Wellington Street. It was not as grand as their first place of employment, but the owners were warm, friendly people and the sisters felt at home immediately. Horse-drawn carriages lined up in the square by the railway station opposite, and tethering posts on the Wellington Street frontage were in constant use as thirsty riders came and went.

Mary and Daisy were earning £1.10.0 a week. The wage included their board and lodging and they knew they were far better off than paying for accommodation elsewhere. They settled into life in Perth, and arrangements to join a ship and return to England kept being deferred for one reason or another, until the matter ceased to be mentioned at all. It was accepted that they had reached their new home.[4]

Not long after arriving in Perth they sought out a distant cousin on their father's side of the family. Frederick (Fred) John Carter had been brought out from England by the D'Oyly Carte musical comedy company. He was a professional singer of some note and performed with the company in the eastern States for several years before moving to Western Australia. When Mary and Daisy came into his life, Fred, a civil servant, was a widower with three children. Soon after their meeting a romance developed between Daisy and Fred, nurtured no doubt, by their common interest in music. Daisy shared Mary's talent for singing and dancing and became involved in the local D'Oyly Carte Company, of which Fred was already a member.[5] They married at St. Albans Anglican Church on 11 December 1902. Thus Daisy changed her status but not her surname.

On her marriage Daisy acquired a family of three and, during the next six years, two daughters and one son were born to her and Fred - Millicent Ailsa, Irene Elsie and Frederick Ernest. The marriage appears to have been a happy one, but of short duration. Fred was injured in a railway accident and died some time prior to 1914, leaving Daisy to bring up six children.[6] This she did with the same industry and determination as her sister Mary showed in building a business empire.

Later in her life, Daisy remarried but stayed only briefly with her new partner. She remained very close to Mary and was a casual helper at the Wentworth when I first met her in 1948. Daisy died in 1967 following a fall at her home in Mount Lawley. She was aged eighty-nine.[7]

Mary found that she could save £1.7.6 from her meagre weekly income.[8] The frugal habits that made this possible stayed with her throughout her life.

Now confident of her ability to keep earning, Mary decided it was time to put to work the £100 she had held onto through thick and thin.

Sunday was her day off. For Mary, the most enjoyable way to spend the day was looking at houses and land that were advertised for sale, and she always dreamed of the day when she would have saved enough to make a purchase. One Sunday afternoon in April 1903, Mary went to inspect a house she had noticed for sale in Subiaco. The address was the corner of Townsend Road and Perth Street - now Churchill Road. The property, number 73, remains today, the only building of the four corner locations to have survived redevelopment. The asking price was £450, and Mary saw it as a good investment - a property close to the city, and one which would not be difficult to keep tenanted. Adding her savings to the precious £100, she put down a deposit of £220 and borrowed the balance from Mr John McGinn, a Perth civil servant. The mortgage, showing an interest rate of seven per cent, was registered on 22 July 1903. Mary lost no time in installing a tenant, charging £1.5.0 rent per week, and was in no doubt that her acquisition would be quickly paid for. Indeed, the mortgage was discharged on 31 July 1905.

For the first time, Mary had put into practice the credo on which she was to build an empire - *Always be in debt. It is the only way to make money.* I doubt that she would have approved being in debt to the extent of the Bonds and Connells of the 1980s, but the theory certainly worked for her. As soon as one property was almost paid off, she would move on to her next investment. Her second venture was to acquire the vacant land adjoining the Townsend Road property and to build a house on it. This cost £350 and the weekly return was £1.5.0.

Mary retained her interest in music and theatre. Although her voice had lost much of its special quality, she still loved to sing and joined the choir at the Wesley Church in William Street. Here she was chosen to render the solo anthem at Sunday services. Some of the congregation were not entirely happy to have a barmaid singing solo in their church, but Mary had her supporters and refused to let her critics spoil the pleasure she got from performing.[9]

On an outing to the Theatre Royal, Mary met William Morris Thomas, a civil servant who lived in Golden Street, North Perth. He was tall, with strong even features and the look of a man who spent a lot of time outdoors. He upheld the tradition of his Irish forebears by displaying an entertaining gift of the gab and was often the centre of a group enjoying his wit and banter. Bill, as he was known, had noticed the tall blond girl behind the bar at the Central Hotel, but was intimidated by her no nonsense approach and reluctance to engage in the kind of familiar small talk most barmaids served up with the beer. With a formal introduction to bolster his confidence, Bill pursued Mary with determination

It was a turbulent courtship, his drinking habits being a constant source of friction. Even so, Mary found herself falling in love with her charming suitor. Against her better judgment, she did eventually say 'Yes', and wedding plans advanced to the stage where the banns appeared on the notice board of the Wesley Church. Then, within days of the big event, Bill forgot the promise to curtail his drinking. Mary was furious and a very serious quarrel resulted in the cancellation of all arrangements. Undaunted, Bill refused to take 'No' for an answer. As Mary told the story - she was on duty at the Central when he stormed into the bar, paid an off-duty barman to work her shift, and carried her off to obtain a special licence and marry him at the Registry Office. The wedding date was 5 May 1905. Mary took a day off for the honeymoon then went back to work at the hotel whilst Bill returned to his job in the country.[10]

Bill had worked for a time on a property in the Harvey district and harboured an ambition to try his luck on the land. He was convinced that with the right wife by his side he could make make a go of it.

At first Mary was reluctant to leave Perth. Her small investments were proving successful and her job at the Central was secure. However, she had married to be with her husband and to support him in building a life together. Bill convinced her that he could see a secure future for them in farming and Mary put aside her own interests to return to the Harvey property with him.

The house to which Bill Thomas took Mary had started out as a typical farming cottage of the era, but spasmodic occupation had allowed nature to move in and reclaim the space and it was a tumble-down version of what it had once been. A rough timber frame surrounded the basic interior, which was divided into three sections for sleeping, eating and cooking. Bathing and laundry facilities were located in a lean-to behind the house, and the lavatory stood in isolation some distance away. A verandah along the front and one side of the building gave the illusion of a more spacious interior, whilst the sprawling tin roof completed the deception.

It was all far removed from what a new bride might have dreamed of. It meant living rough in the truest sense of the word. By comparison, the basic live-in accommodation at the Central was actually palatial! However, Mary refused to be discouraged, and was determined to make a success of their venture. There was no lack of enthusiasm as she and Bill set about clearing land and planting wheat.

The first crop flourished and the promise of a good season's return made the hardship and discomfort easier to bear. They greeted each day with optimism. The wheat matured - a sea of glossy green fronds reaching upwards. Then disaster struck. Kangaroos moved in like an invading army, as if they had been waiting for the precise time when the crop would be at its most juicy and succulent. Bill and Mary tried desperately to keep the marauders at bay. It was hopeless. Fires lit at night to frighten the enemy off, seemed only to make it easier for the 'roos to locate the best patches.[11]

Mary had married with the same hopes and dreams as brides of every generation. These dreams included having a family. Her longing for a child dominated the early years of her marriage. Why didn't she become pregnant? Her mother was forever pregnant when she didn't want to be and here she was, apparently unable to conceive! The obvious thing was to see a doctor. Many years later, when Mary had long forgotten her maternal yearnings, she found the episode highly amusing.

> After a lengthy examination and much questioning, the doctor said that today would be the perfect date to allow nature to do its best work. 'Go home now. Find your husband, and get to it.' As usual, the bugger was nowhere to be found![12]

In light of subsequent events it was probably fortunate that her hopes were not realised, but at the time her failure to become pregnant caused sadness and disappointment.

The birth of a child of her own was a joy Mary was not destined to experience. Ailsa Raymond of Kingsley, Daisy's granddaughter, recalls that the family was aware that Mary was desperate to become a mother. Daisy often sent Millicent, Ailsa's mother, the eldest of her three children, to stay with Aunt Mary and Uncle Bill at their farm in Harvey. Millicent remained a firm favourite with Mary throughout her life.[13]

Meanwhile bad seasons and failed crops continued to thwart every effort Bill and Mary made to get the farm running successfully. The small returns were causing such financial hardship that when Mary heard a boarding house in nearby Mornington Mills was up for lease, she suggested to Bill that she take it on until things got better. The residential, with only six guest rooms, was a very small business and required a lot of hard work, but at least, it brought in an income. It was a sensible short term solution to their problems and

Mary began to share her days between the farm and the boarding house.

Morgan Smith of Australind had an amusing story to tell about Mary Thomas.

> My father lived and worked at Mornington Mills at the time Mary Thomas ran a small boarding house in the town. Mill workers used to stay there. Even then, she was an identity. She was a bigger person than in her later years - quite buxom. According to my father, on very hot days she would carry a towel to keep perspiration at bay, and with no inhibitions at all would unbutton her blouse and dab away - much to the delight of the youths of the village.[14]

The more she thought about it, the more Mary came to the realisation that the uncertainties of farming were not for her. She started to have serious misgivings and to question the common sense of continuing to fight what had become a losing battle.

As is often the case a small, even amusing incident, was the last straw. Working through intermittent rain one day in late autumn of 1911, Mary found that her clothing was soaked. When she finally went to bed, Bill hung her clothes beside the glowing wood stove to dry overnight. They caught fire and were burned to ashes. Quite literally, Mary had nothing to wear! She had left some clothes at the boarding house in Mornington Mills and, to cover herself until she got there, used a wheat sack to make a skirt, and another was converted into a top by cutting out slits for the neck and armholes![15]

The upshot of this fiasco, added to the other failed endeavours, was that Mary decided to return to the city, leaving Bill to continue his battle against nature and the kangaroos. The farming venture at Harvey only ever enjoyed moderate success. Eventually Bill turned to cattle dealing as a more secure source of income.

The marriage barely survived its inauspicious start and Mary, in referring to those times, never suggested that it had been a happy union. However, she would not have left the marriage had the failure of their farming enterprise been the only concern. There were personal difficulties, not the least being Bill's fondness for alcohol, which was increasing rather than ceasing, as he had promised.

Mary accepted that she should put it all behind her and try to pick up the threads of her previous life in Perth, without taking the final step of seeking a divorce. She moved into a house at 121 Newcastle Street, Perth, which she had bought before she married and had kept tenanted to pay off the mortgage. Bill stayed there with her on rare occasions when he visited the city, but he continued to spend most of his time on the Harvey farm.

One day in 1918, whilst Bill was riding towards the Harvey Hotel, his horse put its front hooves into a hidden pothole. It stumbled, he slipped from the saddle and the horse fell heavily on top of him. Help arrived quickly and he was taken to the Harvey Hotel, there being no hospital in the area, but nothing could be done. Bill had broken his neck.[16] Guy Palmer of Harvey recalls his father telling him of the incident, and more details of the tragedy were recorded in tapes of Harvey's history left by the late, well known local identity, Lou Fryer. The publican's daughter asked Bill if he would like her to play the piano for him. 'Please,' he replied. 'Play "When I Leave The World Behind".'

Mary hurried to his side when she heard news of the accident, but arrived too late to say goodbye. Bill Thomas is buried in Cookernup Cemetery, some fourteen kilometres north of Harvey.[17] It is interesting that this was the site originally chosen for the town, the cemetery having already been established before a better position was decided on. The farm where Bill and Mary battled so gamely, now lies in the middle of the Harvey Weir, some fifty feet under water. Mary found it ironic that Bill should have been thrown from his horse and killed on one of the rare occasions when he was sober.[18]

When Mary returned to Perth she set about making up for lost time. Work was not difficult to come by and she found employment as a barmaid at a city hotel, promising herself that this would be for a short time only. Mary resumed her drive to acquire property, concentrating on modest investments in land and housing and sticking to the formula she had already found to be successful. Purchases in Subiaco, East Perth and Perth itself were turned over relatively quickly, always at a profit, which provided the deposit for the next venture. However, working and saving as an employee was too slow for Mary, and she was intent on acquiring a business of her own.

Early in 1912, not long after she returned to Perth from Harvey, Mary received the grim news that her mother was suffering from cancer and was terminally ill. She was devastated. She decided she must go home. The sadness of the occasion negated the natural excitement she felt in seeing her family and her homeland for the first time in twelve years. It was a source of great sorrow to Mary that her mother, at the age of 57, passed away before she arrived.[19]

A very positive outcome from the visit was that she persuaded two of her brothers, George and Fred, to follow in her footsteps and settle in Perth. Both were considerably younger than Mary, being almost the last-born of the family. George subsequently became Mary's right hand man and was actively engaged in many of her business ventures. He worked with her at the Wentworth and managed the Bohemia for many years, as well as helping her to set up other hotel acquisitions as they came along. Fred was quick to identify with his adopted country, answering the call to enlist in 1914 when he was only just old enough to do so. He fought with the Anzac forces at Gallipoli and, after the war, worked as an engine driver with Government Rail. He later turned to poultry farming in Osborne Park and established a viable enterprise.[20]

In 1926, Fred joined Mary in a partnership to buy the Red Lion Hotel and remained as its licensee until December 1931. He then decided to try his hand at farming, a venture in which he was very successful. Fred returned to the liquor industry in the early 1950s. For a time he ran the Alhambra Bars on the corner of Hay and Barrack Streets, before taking over the Newmarket Hotel from his brother George in 1953. He remained the licensee until the hotel closed and was demolished in the 1960s. Fred Carter was reputed to have been an excellent hotel keeper. He retired at seventy-six and died aged eighty-two. His granddaughter, Glenys Rosling, born in 1949, has happy memories of running riot in the Wentworth kitchen and great-aunt Mary didn't seem to mind at all![21]

Returning to Perth after visiting her home, Mary renewed her search for a suitable business venture. The opportunity presented itself in 1915 when a cafe in William Street was offered for sale. Owned by John Lofthouse and located on the eastern side of William Street, between Hay and Murray Streets, it was called the Bon Ton Cafe. It was in the right position to attract workers from the surrounding commercial block as well as city shoppers. Before committing herself to the purchase Mary positioned herself for some time each day to observe the customers' comings and goings. When she had satisfied herself that the business looked promising, and feeling confident that she could do better than the then owner, Mary paid a deposit and in due course became the new proprietor.[22] This was her biggest challenge to date. Success or failure depended on her.

A good scrub worked wonders for the premises and, with a new menu on offer, business was brisk from the very first day. The house special was a meal of fish served with bread, butter and tea, for ninepence. Pies cost threepence, pasties twopence.[23] The business prospered. The venture was so successful that Mary purchased a second cafe in the same street. Situated on the western side, between Murray and Wellington Streets, it was called the Popular Cafe, and Mary placed it under management. On one occasion a customer who had purchased meat pies returned them, claiming they were mouldy. The manager refused to offer replacements and the customer took his complaint to the Perth City Council health inspector. Prosecution followed and the manager was fined £10.0.0. Meanwhile, he had gone to England leaving the fine unpaid. Because Mary owned the cafe and employed the manager, the council's officer called on her to pay the fine.

'Why come to me?' she asked. 'It wasn't me who was fined.'

'But the manager's gone to England,' he said.

Her response - 'Well, you'll have to go to England for your £10.0.0, won't you?' The newspapers jokingly referred to the incident as the case of the mouldy pie. Rightly or wrongly, Mary never did pay up and years later she would chuckle with satisfaction remembering her victory over bureaucracy.[24]

Soon after she bought the Bon Ton Cafe, Mary met Abraham Joseph Krakouer, who owned a wine saloon at 134 William Street, close to the Popular Cafe. His great-niece, Terri-ann White of Perth, recalls that there is general acceptance within her family, that her great-uncle and Mary Thomas had a relationship spanning several years, although he was twenty-four years her senior.[25]

Abraham Krakouer was born in 1853, the first child of Theodore and Brina Krakouer. He was also the first Jewish baby born in Fremantle. In 1851, Theodore had been transported from England for stealing money and clothing, but he soon became a ticket-of-leave man and began operating a livery stable.[26]

Abraham's early working life was spent as a teamster, travelling between Perth and Albany and later, supplying food and liquor to the Coolgardie diggings. At the time he worked out of Williams, where he employed three men.

Elizabeth Williams of Mt Lawley, Abraham Krakouer's great-granddaughter, shared with me the following information she has collated whilst researching her family history.

> In 1881 my great- grandfather married Alicia Catherine Robinson, with whom he fathered seven children. It was during the time of this marriage, in 1885, that Abraham was charged with the murder of Henry Rodber, a sailor from the ship *Diamond*. Within the family, the story goes that Abraham returned home and discovered that the sailor had been showing his wife undue attention. An altercation developed and Abraham shot him dead. However, the case may not have been as cut and dried as it sounds. Abraham claimed to have shot the man in self defence, was sentenced for manslaughter and spent two years in custody on Rottnest Island.[27]

Abraham's wife died in 1894. In the mid 1890s, in partnership with his brothers, Rudolph and Raphael, Abraham built and operated hotels in Coolgardie, Norseman and Collie, where he became a member of the local council and finally, the mayor.[28] He bought the wine saloon in William Street the year before Mary bought the Bon Ton Cafe.

Abraham remarried in 1896. His bride was Mary Alexandra Montague, daughter of a prestigious British family and she came

Courtesy Ailsa Raymond

Mary Raine (2nd left) with her sisters - visit to UK in 1922

out to Australia expressly to marry Abraham. There was one son from the marriage. In 1917, in partnership with his wife, Abraham took over the Great Western Hotel, across the railway line on the north-west corner of William Street. Mary Alexandra died from kidney disease in 1920.[29]

Mary Raine's niece, Ailsa Raymond, remembers Abraham Krakouer's name coming up in family conversation over the years, and she always had the impression that he was a cultured and valued friend. His name appears on sheet music which came into Ailsa's possession after Mary's death.[30] Abraham is reputed to have had an excellent singing voice,[31] and no doubt he and Mary could have found a bond through their shared interest in music. They would also have been on common ground through the liquor industry, in which he was engaged, and in which Mary had worked for many years before buying the Bon Ton Cafe.

Zoe Garbutt (nee Krakouer) granddaughter of Abraham Krakouer, tells the following unverified story, which she heard on many occasions from her mother, Rebecca, his daughter-in-law.

> When Mary Raine, or Mary Thomas as she was at the time, returned to England to visit her family in 1925, my grandfather remarried for the third time, and left the Gordons (later Wentworth) Hotel to live with his new wife at the Great Western Hotel over the railway line in William Street. When Mary returned she was so furious she threw clothes he had left at the Gordons Hotel out of the upstairs window and onto the street below. My mother said the incident was the talk of Perth. [32]

I have no difficulty in believing the incident happened. Years later when I knew her, Mary had a fiery temper, and it would have been courting disaster to double-cross her. It is certain that in 1925 the electoral roll shows Abraham Krakouer's address as the Gordons Hotel, even though it was the year in which he married his third wife, Elizabeth Gertrude Krakouer, widow of his brother Rudolph. Abraham died in 1928, and two years later, Elizabeth married Herbert Keyser.

It is reasonable to wonder why Mary and Abraham did not choose to marry, since both were free to do so, and there is evidence of a lasting relationship spanning some ten years. This started during the time of Abraham's marriage to Mary Alexandra and continued beyond her death in 1920.

It would seem that Mary forgave Abraham for his betrayal. When he died in May 1928 her tribute, published in *The West Australian* read:

> Abraham Joseph Krakouer: At Perth Hospital, after a short illness, most beloved friend of Mary B Thomas.
> 'God giveth his most beloved rest.'

Mary's relationship with Abraham Krakouer's family was not affected by his unexpected marriage to someone else. His daughter Rebecca, who was living and working at the Wentworth, continued to do so until the late 1940s. Years later, when Rebecca's daughter, Zoe Garbutt, was employed at Foy and Gibson in Hay Street, Mary allowed her to park her car behind the hotel, and didn't object when the chef gave Zoe samples from the menu.[33]

Terri-ann White, Zoe Garbutt and Ailsa Raymond remember a large framed portrait of Abraham Krakouer that hung on the wall behind the reception desk at the Wentworth for many years.[34] It was not there in 1948, and I have not been able to establish what has become of it, but it is logical to assume that the portrait would have been removed after Mary married Joe in 1943.

Mary ran the Bon Ton Cafe for eight years, during which time she continued to invest in land. Recognising East Perth's potential as a residential area she also built a small row of houses. The work was undertaken by sub-contractors under Mary's direction and supervision. Her real estate holdings continued to grow.

Mary also recognised a business opportunity when men, returning from World War 1 were looking for ways to establish themselves in civilian life. As a gift from a grateful nation, the men were given bonds, or gratuities, as they were called. The bonds were of no immediate use as they did not mature for three years and the men needed money there and then. Most resorted to money-lenders, who were redeeming the bonds for a twenty per cent fee, and when Mary was approached by some of her customers, she cashed about ten for considerably less. She received a call from the Treasury Department and was advised that she needed a permit to cash war bonds. She was encouraged to apply for one, to cover the bonds already cashed and any future transactions. Mary sensed the Department was pleased to see some competition for the money-lenders that could lead to a reduction in the amount of commission the men were paying.[35]

With the disappearance of recruiting and war bond posters, button sellers, casualty lists and battle maps from outside newspaper offices, the gloomy war years were quickly forgotten. Australia was ready to move on. Even the threat of Spanish 'flu, which had been brought from Europe by returning servicemen and would eventually claim 11,000 Australian lives, did not dampen the prevailing feeling of optimism.

The Bon Ton Cafe prospered during the war years and provided a sound income to fund Mary's property investments. Unfortunately, there was a temporary setback to this situation when a fire broke out on Friday 14 June 1921 at the Economic Department Store on the corner of Hay and William Streets and spread to the adjacent Bon Ton Cafe. Firemen battled to halt the fast spreading flames, and only the blessing of an easterly wind saved the loss of all the businesses in the street. Even so, Mary's cafe was extensively damaged. When repairs had been completed, she began to think very seriously of selling the business and directing her energies into a more substantial undertaking.

In 1921, for a woman of Mary's confidence and foresight, Western Australia was the right place to be.

The State had the honour of being the first in the Federation to elect a woman to its legislature. Mrs Edith Cowan, MLA for West Perth addressed the Legislative Assembly of Western Australia on 28th July 1921, stressing the importance of her role in representing all women and accepting that she had been elected to the Assembly to remind men of all that needed to be done for home and family.

Later the same year saw Western Australia leading the way in another important area. West Australian Airways Ltd was established by Major Norman Brearley, Mr L Taplin and Mr C Kingsford-Smith for the purpose of servicing Commonwealth Government mail-carrying contracts in the far north of the State. Announcement of the exciting new venture, starting between Geraldton and Broome, was greeted with great public enthusiasm, and seen as the forerunner to extended commercial airline services. Sadly, the inaugural flight on 30 October 1921, was marred by tragedy when one of the Bristol aircraft crashed, killing its pilot, Lt Robert Fawcett and his mechanic, Edward Broad. It was fortunate that the inauspicious start did not adversely affect public acceptance of the new service.

It is interesting to look back on Perth city in the early 1920s. The following information has been gleaned from studying the advertising section of *The West Australian* of the time. The male basic wage was £150 per year for a single man. The married rate was £182. The average family home could be bought for £400. Mansions on about an acre of land would cost some £2,000, whilst a four-room house close to the river in Claremont could be rented for about £1.0.0 per week. A man's three-piece suit cost £5.0.0, a woman's dress £1.10.0, a woman's suit £2.10.0. Beer cost sixpence a pint, an outing to the pictures one shilling for adults, sixpence for children. Boans Family Department Store advertised a vocal and orchestral concert to be held in the Tea and Luncheon Rooms each Wednesday from 3.00 p.m - 5.00 p.m. Mills and Wares Company extolled the virtues of Milk Arrowroot Biscuits 'made only from milk, sugar and wheat' - a gift coupon in each package. A Mary Pickford movie was showing at The Palladium in Fremantle, a photo of the star being given away to each child paying for admission.

The so-called 'flapper' era, decreeing short cropped hair and short fringed dresses, had ushered in a new freedom for women. This was, arguably, the first time young women had proclaimed their own special place in the scheme of things. They were more vocal, more strident and more self-assured than ever before and the clock would never be turned back.

About this time, Mary again visited her family in England. On this occasion she was able to report significant success in acquiring and running her own cafes, as well as adding to her property portfolio.

Fred and George were both doing well and the remaining members of Mary's family were eager to hear about business opportunities in Perth.

Over the years, Mary made many more visits to her homeland and eventually persuaded all but two of her surviving brothers and sisters to come to Western Australia. During the 1930s her sisters Florence Maude (Toby) and Gertrude May (Gertie), who was suffering the aftermath of a broken marriage, succumbed to Mary's urging and settled in Perth. Unfortunately, Gertie was diagnosed with cancer quite soon afterwards and died in 1934. Within a short time the sisters were followed by the youngest member of the family, John Felix (Jack) Carter and his wife Dora. Mary found positions for all within her growing empire.

For some time Mary had been watching a property situated on the northwest corner of William and Murray Streets, diagonally opposite the Bon Ton Cafe. It was in an ideal position and, most importantly, it was licensed to serve wine and beer with meals. The business was popularly known as the Gordons Hotel, being leased by a man of that name, but it was registered as the Cafe Anglais. To avoid confusion in the telling of these events it will be referred to as the Gordons Hotel. In 1922 the property became part of a deceased estate - the Williams estate - and an astute agent by the name of O'Dea let Mary know it was for sale.[36]

Without hesitation Mary made an offer of £30,000 and pressured the agent to get the deal finalised before the property's availability was widely publicised. However, there was a problem. One of the owners was a minor, and the sale had to be approved by the Supreme Court. This took time. During the enforced delay another interested party, a wealthy pastoralist, made an offer of £40,000 on a deposit of £2,000. The solicitor for the vendors suggested to Mary that if she wanted the property she should match the offer and increase the deposit to £5,000. This she did, and the Gordons Hotel was hers - or almost.

Mary would not have bought with such confidence but for the fact that a moneylender with whom she had dealt previously had encouraged her, on his undertaking to take a fifty per cent share himself. It was an agreement made only on a handshake and she was fully committed to the purchase when he withdrew his offer, leaving Mary with a serious problem. The deposit was in place from profits made by cashing wartime gratuities, but where was she to borrow the balance? Her capital was tied up in mortgaged properties and she had hoped to acquire the Gordons Hotel without sacrificing existing investments.[37]

Mary walked the length of St George's Terrace, canvassing lending institutions without success or even a glimmer of hope. The fact that she was a woman on her own outweighed all other considerations. Her successful cafe businesses, her record of mortgages paid out well in advance of the due date, meant nothing. Grim-faced men behind cluttered desks in gloomy offices scarcely allowed her time to plead her case. She couldn't give up. Her persistence won out when the manager of the National Mutual Company politely ushered her into his office and listened attentively to what she had to say. Impressed by her confidence and her excellent record of business successes, he offered the backing she so desperately needed. The loan was for £20,000. Some small properties were sold to provide the balance of money required.[38] The association with the National Mutual was to continue throughout Mary's business life and the company had cause to be pleased that one of its managers recognised a gilt-edged investment when he saw one.

The purchase of the Gordons Hotel was significant. It was Mary's first major investment. The sale was finalised early in 1924 and the liquor licence transferred to her name on 5 March the same year. The acquisition came at a time when Australia in general and Western Australia in particular, were caught in a postwar property boom. The wheeling and dealing of the 1980s would be reminiscent of these times - demand outstripping supply and pushing up prices. Perth's citizens were ready to forge a brave new world. Those with a sharp eye for opportunities quickly emerged to lead the vanguard, and Mary Thomas was one of them.

Chapter 4

Speculate to accumulate

1924 - 1939

When Mary Thomas took the helm at the Gordons Hotel on 5 March 1924, business improved significantly. Her brother, George, was employed to share the management, leaving Mary with some free time to develop other interests. A niece, Mary Coward of Bullcreek, remembers George as a quiet, calmly efficient man, the perfect non-competitive lieutenant for someone as self-determined as his sister.[1] He came to be highly regarded in the hotel industry and never wavered in his devotion to Mary.

Prior to taking over the Gordons Hotel, Mary established Metropolitan Properties Ltd to control her growing real estate portfolio. The company was registered on 14 February 1924, with a capital of £100,000 in £1.0.0 shares. At that early stage most of the shares remained unissued. To conform with legal requirement that there should be at least five shareholders, the original issue was as follows:

Millicent Ailsa Carter (Daisy's daughter)	1 share
Sydney Frederick Carter (Fred - Mary's brother)	1 share
Brian George Carter (George - Mary's brother)	1 share
Valentine Rutherford Abbott (Mary's solicitor)	1 share
Mary Bertha Thomas	1000 shares

William Toy, a high profile Perth real estate agent was always on the lookout for suitable properties to offer Mary, and a large number of investments were made at this time. Many were resold quickly, and always at a profit. The old State Implement and

Engineering Works in Murray Street was acquired soon after the formation of the new company. Mary paid £13,500 for it, on a deposit of £1,500, and arranged to pay the balance on terms. An agent, commissioned to invest money for a Jewish Rabbi, offered her £14,000 soon after purchase. There was no capital gains tax in those days and Mary, a great believer in taking a quick profit if it was on offer, accepted. The Rabbi was on holiday at the time the deal was made and was not pleased with the purchase when he returned to inspect it. He insisted on reselling immediately and lost about £2,000 on the deal.[2]

Over a relatively short period, Mary acquired several significant properties, among them a number of shops in William Street, adjacent to the Gordons Hotel, but her main interest was in hotel ownership. In 1926, in partnership with her brother Fred, she bought the Union Hotel in Aberdeen Street, North Perth. The hotel was renamed the Red Lion, then became the Aberdeen Hotel; today it is known simply as The Deen. The hotel was built in 1911, and Mary paid £31,000 for it. George and his wife, Nellie, took over as managers on 8 January 1927, until Fred assumed control on 25 May 1928. Mary subsequently sold her share of the freehold, but Fred retained his share until 11 December 1931.

Meanwhile, under Mary's energetic guidance, the Gordons Hotel continued to prosper. Although it was the first time she had held a liquor licence in her own name, she was no stranger to the obligations the licence carried, nor to the best way to extract good business from the privilege of having it. After all, she had served a punishing apprenticeship at the Nyngan Hotel and learned a lot from it. The Gordons Hotel fulfilled the promise Mary had so confidently expected, and she set her mind to implementing the ambitious plans she had for it.

Financial advisers might have suggested it was not a good time to be taking on debt or developing a business venture, but Mary thought otherwise. Early in 1927, defying the rumblings of the approaching Depression, she contacted the National Mutual Company which held a mortgage over the Gordons Hotel. She needed funds to rebuild the premises to the standard required to upgrade the Wine and Beer Licence to a Publican's General Licence. This was an ambitious undertaking, requiring major additions and alterations to the existing building.

The National Mutual Company agreed to advance £18,000. With the plan approved and the necessary building permits in place, Mary immersed herself in the project, calling on the experience she had gained whilst building the row of houses in Bennett Street, East Perth. The new hotel's style has since come to be known as inter-war free classical. The work added forty bedrooms, some balconies, guests' lounges and a commercial room, as well as replacing existing bars, drinking lounges, dining room and kitchen. The estimated cost of building and refurbishing was £27,000.

To ensure that everything was done as she wanted, Mary was on site daily. The building was completed in 1928 and she renamed it the Wentworth Hotel, after a successful hotel of that name in Sydney, also owned by a woman, Mrs Hannah Maclurcan. Along with running a large hotel, this industrious lady wrote cookery books and published The Wentworth Magazine as a means to promote her hotel. Hannah Maclurcan and Mary Thomas had more in common than the name of their hotels. Both were entrepreneurial forward thinkers, ahead of their time, and both recognised that there was an important ingredient needed for success. Hannah Maclurcan offered 'service and luxury', Mary Thomas promised 'service and affordability'.[3]

Replacing the existing Wine and Beer Licence with a Publican's General Licence proved to be more than a mere formality. Mary's first application was unsuccessful, as was the second. No explanation was given and she was at a loss to understand why, having spent so much money on upgrading the premises, she was being denied a full liquor licence. No doubt the Court had received objections from hotel proprietors in the immediate vicinity, and these would not have welcomed another competitor. However, Mary persevered and was rewarded on her third application.[4]

After the Licensing Court had inspected the premises, the Chairman, Mr Cahill was enthusiastic in praising Mary for her foresight in focusing the new hotel on the needs of country people.

> 'We desire to congratulate Mrs Thomas on her enterprise,' said Mr Cahill. 'The Bench is quite satisfied that this is going to be a splendid hotel, and will cater for a section of the community that should be catered for - the hard-working people in the country when they pay a visit to Perth. On the tariff to be charged the hotel should be very well patronised by very deserving clients.' He wished Mrs Thomas every success in her enterprise. [5]

The fully-licensed Hotel Wentworth opened on 19 November 1928. It became Mary's whole world and the flagship of her business empire. 'Ma Thomas' or simply 'Ma', as she had come to be called by customers and staff, was already recognised as a Perth identity.

The new Wentworth had a lot to offer and soon became a Perth landmark. The hotel made no claim to be smart or sophisticated. As promised in the licensing application, it was a people's hotel, a watering hole for the man in the street and as such, enjoyed enormous popularity. Crowds patronised the roomy bars and comfortable lounge every night of the week, and on Fridays and Saturdays late arrivals missed out on a table. The fact that the Wentworth was the only lounge in Perth offering live musical entertainment, was a big drawcard. Reasonable dress standards were enforced in the lounge. Mary would never have imagined a time when it would be necessary for hotels to display signs stating 'No T-shirts or sandals'! Service was the key word. Woe betide the stewardess who had not whisked away an empty glass to be refilled, before Mary's eagle eye lit on it!

Country visitors were quick to avail themselves of the very reasonable tariff and excellent dining room. These patrons remained loyal to the Wentworth for decades and the hotel boasted an average occupancy rate of ninety per cent.

Even though it was not yet evident that a world-wide Depression was looming, this was not a good time for business. Many ventures came to grief and hotels were by no means immune to failure. Mary decided it would be prudent to consolidate her real estate portfolio by disposing of some of her smaller properties and concentrating on acquiring hotels.

Even today, the auction of so many city properties, placed on the market by one vendor, would cause a stir in real estate circles.

Courtesy The West Australian

Wentworth Hotel, circa 1930

The lots offered comprised seven single-storey brick shops on the corner of Roe and William Streets, sold to Mr W Montgomery for £13,500, inner city properties, sold to Cecil Dent Ltd for £11,440, the Wembley Buildings in Hay Street East, sold for £5,250, and 'Ettawanda', in Mounts Bay Road, which realised £3,000. Private residences in Adelaide Terrace, Bennett and Newcastle Streets, brought a total of £3,200.[6]

In all, the sale returned £36,380, and placed Metropolitan Properties in a sound position to weather whatever financial storms might lie ahead. Mary prepared to make 1928 a very busy year.

Before the Wentworth was completed, a small hotel next to it on the Murray Street frontage, came onto the market. It was not new, but during 1928 as work progressed on the neighbouring Wentworth Hotel, extensive alterations had been made.

Little of the hotel's early history is known, but an interesting photograph in the records of *The West Australian* shows a handsome building, decorated with flags to celebrate the visit of the Duke and Duchess of York. It is dated 1901 and captioned 'Jacoby's Bohemia Hotel'. An eye-catching feature is the strikingly beautiful iron lace decorating the street overhang from the second floor balcony, repeated again to surround the roof on the Murray Street frontage. The hotel was built on the site of what had been Glyde and Sons grocery store. Briefly known as the Cafe de Paris, the name was later changed to the Bohemia Hotel.

The alterations made the building less ornate but probably more practical. The design, since described as inter-war functionalist, conformed with popular hotel architecture of the time.

The proximity of this competitor gave Mary cause for concern. When the refurbished hotel was advertised for sale, she had to accept that it posed a threat to the Wentworth bar trade. It was much too close for comfort and there was always the possibility that a live-wire new owner could present real competition. The asking price was £40,500. Mary approached the National Mutual Company again, and was elated to receive the manager's unqualified support.[7] The

Courtesy The West Australian

United Service Hotel 1920s

Courtesy The West Australian

United Service Hotel 1958

purchase was completed in June 1928, and on the fifteenth of that month the ever-dependable George took over as manager. The arrangement worked out well without either business being a threat to the other.

Everything was running smoothly, then something happened to suggest George's tenure at the Bohemia would be brief. A representative of J C Williamson's Theatre Company approached Mary to discuss the possibility of purchasing the hotel to convert it into a theatre.[8]

'What do you think?' Mary asked her brother

It was an unfair question to ask George so soon after he had taken on the licence, and in replying he tried to be objective.

'Of course, it's up to you, but my advice is to hold onto it, unless you can do really well out of a sale.'

However, the more Mary thought about it, the more she liked the idea of having a theatre next to the Wentworth. It would be good for business, and in any case, she would pick up the trade from the Bohemia once it closed. After lengthy discussion, Mary agreed to give the company an option to purchase for £46,000, an option that could be exercised in four years, on condition that a theatre would then be built on the site. It was only a matter of months since she had bought the hotel and the price represented a worthwhile profit. The J C Williamson Company lodged a deposit of £10,000.[9]

Without hesitation, Mary looked around for an investment to replace the Bohemia, having in mind that she wanted to be able to offer George another licence. The King Edward Hotel on the corner of Pier and Hay Streets had recently come on the market. Mary had been very tempted to make an offer, but with so much current concern about the state of the world's economy, decided it would be unwise to take on another substantial commitment. However, circumstances had now changed. She would simply exchange one investment for another. Her offer of £42,000 on the King Edward Hotel was accepted and she paid a deposit of £10,000.

The deepening gloom of the Depression was beginning to keep crowds away from performances of J C Williamson's Company. It was impossible to ignore the situation, and the Company made the difficult decision to withdraw its offer on the Bohemia and lose the deposit. Mary had never considered the possibility of the sale falling through. Now she faced the dilemma of being unable to purchase the King Edward. She too, forfeited her deposit.[10] It was the first and only occasion when she had to face a business loss, but the blow was softened by the fact that another party's loss footed the bill.

Mary retained the Bohemia, and the question of parting with it was never raised again. George remained as manager until 1938 when the hotel was leased to a succession of extremely capable hotel keepers. When Mary died in 1960, it was a valuable part of her estate.

Meanwhile the threat of a Depression had become a reality. Such unhappy events are never well-timed and it was unfortunate that this particular social trauma escalated in what had been designated Perth's General Centenary year. In other circumstances, it would have been a time for celebrating the arrival of a new era, whilst looking back on the achievements of the previous hundred years.

Perth was founded by English migrants in 1829, and one hundred years later boasted a population of 200,000. In 1929 it was not only the newest city in the world but also the most remote. The establishment of air links to Melbourne and Sydney in this special year, was symbolic of an end to isolation and for many was the most impressive feature of the centenary. Perth's growing importance was also recognised when it won the right to call its chief functionary the Lord Mayor.

In late October, three weeks after Perth's centennial parade, the New York stock exchange collapsed.

During the two months prior to the collapse, the world economic situation deteriorated rapidly, and Australia quickly felt the impact. The country's economy depended heavily on primary production and those prices were among the first to fall. Wool and wheat prices followed. In the country, thousands of farmers faced the threat of losing their properties, and things were no better in the city. Falling profits meant that businesses were laying off staff and the numbers of unemployed increased daily. Those fortunate enough to have a job were likely to be asked to accept shorter hours if they wanted to keep it.

During the early months, Australian financial journalists were optimistic that the situation would quickly right itself. Unfortunately, the reverse happened. The economic situation deteriorated and unemployment escalated.

With no jobs and no dole the Government introduced a scheme known as 'sustenance', whereby a single man, after a qualifying period, was given two sixpenny meal tickets and a shilling bed ticket daily. The unemployed faced the indignity of queuing up every morning to collect these handouts. The meal tickets could be used at any eating house that offered a meal for the price, and the bed tickets were valid at boarding houses registered with the Government.

Despite ongoing protests over the Government's handling of the crisis, there were no easy solutions. Many of those on the land rode out the storm by resorting to subsistence farming and eating what they grew, but it was more difficult in the cities where unemployment peaked at over thirty per cent in 1932.

Recovery from the effects of the Depression was slow and unspectacular. There was no significant decline in the number of unemployed until after 1933, and another year passed before small businesses started to emerge from the disastrous slump. For many, the privations continued until 1939.

It was amazing that whilst the country was in the grip of stagnation and uncertainty Mary Thomas was able, not only to survive, but to prosper. Years later she explained this with the simple logic that was her recipe for success. 'I cut the profit margins to the bone. My main concern was to keep people coming through the door.'[11]

Keeping people coming through the door of the Wentworth did not divert Mary from adding to her portfolio of properties. Many of her most valuable acquisitions were made during the Depression years. In 1929 she bought the United Service Hotel in St George's Terrace from the Strickland family, for between £50,000 and £60,000, after it had been passed in at auction, when the reserve price of £65,000 was not reached.

The original hotel, reputed to be the first built in Perth, was constructed in 1833. It has been a Premier's lodging, a temporary prison, a semaphore station and the headquarters of the last dingo hunt held in Perth. For many years it was the terminus for Cobb and Co horses and coaches, and one hundred years ago the State's leading race horses were stabled at the rear of the hotel, where horse auctions were held.

In 1895, the hotel was remodelled extensively. Unlike many hotels of that era, the new frontage did not have a balcony overhanging the street - possibly to ensure that it blended unobtrusively into its setting in what was planned to be the main business and professional street of the city. The interesting facade on top of the building featured three panels. One represented the Army, one the Navy, and one was blank. This was prophetic, remembering that flight was in its infancy when construction took place, and no one could have imagined that one day there would be a third arm to the defence forces.

In the early 1950s when my husband and I were working for Mary and her second husband, Joe Raine, I was called on to help them in assessing minor refurbishment necessary at the United Service Hotel. In this way I saw the hotel at close quarters. It was a beautiful building. Of the many interesting features, I best remember the cellars. Joe encouraged visitors to descend the steep stairway and marvel at the quality of the workmanship and materials used in construction. As Joe pointed out, convict labour had been employed for the original work, and even the nails had been hand made.[12]

The United Service Hotel remained in Mary's property portfolio and was part of her bequest to the University of Western Australia in 1960. It was later sold to the Reserve Bank for $160,000, having failed to reach the reserve price at auction. The hotel was demolished in 1968 to make way for The Reserve Bank building which now occupies the position the United Service Hotel once graced on St George's Terrace. What a tragedy that this interesting example of Perth's early history did not survive. Its exit was unheralded and unmourned.

Remembering the public outcry against the demolition of the Old Perth Barracks in 1966, it is amazing that just two years later, a landmark like the United Service Hotel was allowed to vanish into oblivion without a dissenting voice. At the time of the demolition, restoration work was actually in progress on the Barracks Archway at the end of the same street.

Mary did not purchase the United Service Hotel through Metropolitan Properties Ltd, but through a newly registered company which she named the United Service Co Ltd. The same major shareholders, mainly family members who received gifts of shares from Mary, were prominent in both companies.

George took over the management of this latest acquisition and Mary lost no time in moving on to her next investment. This was the Windsor Hotel in South Perth.

The Windsor was built in 1898 for George Strickland at a cost of £4,050. The architect for the project was J Talbot Hobbs, who trained in England. He arrived in Western Australia in 1887, and quickly established a reputation as one of Perth's finest architects. The building was in the free classical style highly favoured at the time, having a wide second floor balcony defined by ornamental iron lace. The freehold of the hotel remained in the Strickland family until 1929 when it was bought by Mary for £25,000.

The Windsor housed South Perth's first Post and Telegraph Office, servicing the area until the volume of business warranted the building of a Post Office on the corner diagonally opposite. The hotel management was also responsible for a paddle-wheel ferry service operating between Perth and the Mends Street jetty. There is no evidence of any alterations or additions being made to the hotel during the years between its construction in 1898 and its sale in 1929.

Author's collection

The Windsor Hotel at the time of purchase in 1928

Author's collection

The Windsor Hotel 1960

Jack Carter and Dora, his wife, together with his sister, Toby, took over the management of the Windsor on 17 June 1929, and the licence remained in one or other of their names for the next sixteen years, until 11 June 1945. Jack may have retired owing to ill-health. He died of a lung-related disease soon after he left the hotel. Mary replaced the family team with a succession of managers. The Windsor Hotel proved to be a very successful addition to Mary's real estate portfolio.

Whilst adding these hotel properties to her empire, Mary was gradually paying off existing mortgages on small city and suburban holdings and acquiring new ones. Important additions were more shops next to the Wentworth on the William Street frontage, continuing on to the Royal Hotel on the corner of Wellington Street. Mary also purchased the Williams Building, directly opposite the Royal. By the time the Depression began to ease in the early 1930s, she held a very significant and valuable section of inner-city real estate and was still extending.

The fact that Mary was able to achieve such a measure of financial success when the country was caught up in a world-wide Depression, was quite remarkable. During these years, simply having a job took on a significance never before appreciated. In the State elections of 1930, the Nationalist-Country Party led by James Mitchell, campaigned on the slogan 'Work for all' and claimed victory from Philip Collier's Labor Party, winning twenty-seven of the fifty-two seats.

Mary's favourite Depression story was to recall a poster the Federal Government asked her to display prominently in her hotels. 'SAVE for your Country's sake', it urged! A year later the request was for her to display a replacement. It exhorted 'SPEND for your Country's sake'.[13]

Pat Garland of Cottesloe kindly sent me *The West Australian's* report of an amusing incident on 20 January 1931 when Mary played a part in saving a bank teller from being mistaken for a bank robber.[14]

Armed with a sandbag, a young man attacked the teller of the Commercial Bank, next to the Wentworth. The teller, though slightly stunned, was able to grab his pistol, and could have hurt the thief, but made sure he only inflicted a flesh wound when he fired. The would-be robber made his escape empty-handed, leaving the teller holding the gun. Others, arriving late on the scene and seeing a man with a gun, assumed he was the thief and pounced on him.

Mary was working in the hotel kitchen, when she heard the shot. She rushed into the bank, where she saw three men struggling on the floor with the teller. She ran into the hotel bar and told men there that the bank teller was being murdered, and returned with them to see the teller being held firmly.

'We've got the thief', one of the captors cried out.

'What's going on?', Mary demanded. 'That's the teller. Let him go.'

In 1936, Mary decided the time was right to implement alterations and refurbishment to the drinking lounge and dining-room of the Wentworth. The existing facilities were no longer large enough to cope with the steadily increasing business. She consulted leading architect, E Le B Henderson, who had been involved in the major rebuilding project in 1928. The work was completed in September of the same year, and the *West Australian Licensed Victuallers' Gazette* described the result in glowing terms.

> An ambitious remodelling and artistic redecorating of the lounges and dining room of the Hotel Wentworth, which proved a test of the skill of the craftsmen and the hotel management to prevent an unsettling of patrons has been completed most expeditiously and with admirable results. This remarkable improvement should be inspected by all interested in catering; a most cursory examination will demonstrate what Mrs. Thomas has obtained in the way of a general and striking advance beyond regulation provisions for service, as well as comfort and convenience for customers.[15]

These alterations served the Wentworth well for twenty-six years. It was 1962, two years after Mary's death, before any further changes were made.

The annual inspection by the Licensing Court prior to relicensing hotel premises was always a time for concern. The officer conducting the inspection had wide-ranging powers. His report could require owners to spend considerable sums of money to correct what he deemed to be shortcomings, or to implement improvements which he considered desirable.

A report from the *W.A.L.V.G.* of December 1936 details the inspection recommendations placed on the United Service Hotel.

> At the sittings of the Licensing Court held to consider applications for the renewal of the annual licences of the metropolitan area hotels this year no applications were refused, (however) in renewing the licence of the United Service Hotel, St George's Terrace, Mr Cahill said the hotel was spotlessly clean and was very well conducted but it provided very little accommodation. In view of the growth of Perth the owner of the hotel should consider whether she could not rebuild the premises within the next year or two. The cost would be great, but the matter called for attention.[16]

Mary was far from pleased when this report reached her. Having spent freely on the Wentworth in the same year, she was not receptive to the suggestion outlined, and chose to ignore it. She was not pressured to comply.[17] No such alterations were ever made to the hotel and, apart from the usual maintenance, it remained unchanged from the date of purchase in 1929 until its demise in 1968.

Late in 1936, Louisa Boom started work at the Wentworth. Her husband had removed himself from the family of two boys and four girls and left his wife to provide for them and bring them up. Fortunately, she was a resourceful lady. Mary Raine, or Mary Thomas, as she was then, offered Mrs Boom a job after she became a tenant in upstairs rooms of a property Mary owned directly opposite the Wentworth.[18] Mrs Boom, a dressmaker, shared the rooms with Belle Gladstone, a milliner who became quite famous in Perth for her wonderful creations and for her slogan - 'Above all, the right hat'.

Mrs Boom's first job for Mary Raine was as housekeeper. She remained until Mary's death in 1960 - a loyal and faithful retainer in the old mould - receptionist, housekeeper, supervisor, seamstress, personal assistant and general factotem. It is difficult to know if any real closeness ever developed between the two women. Over all those years when they worked together day in and day out, they never addressed each other by their Christian names. It was always 'Mrs Raine' and 'Mrs Boom'.

Mrs Boom's services came with what was for Mary, a bonus. The new housekeeper was an accomplished dressmaker and her employer put that talent to good use.

Mary was exceptionally tall. She often told the story of when she was competing at a swimming carnival during her teen years. In position at the edge of the pool, waiting to dive in, she heard a voice yell out. 'Blimey. That's a long 'un!' She was completely put off and swam last, instead of first as she had confidently expected.[19]

Mary's height made it impossible to buy clothes off the rack, and she disliked having to pay the high prices that went with custom-made outfits. It was necessity alone that forced her to become a customer of the Bon Marche dressmaking department, which catered for Perth's wealthiest and most fashionable ladies during the 1930s and beyond. Ruth Williams of Queens Park was a very young apprentice dressmaker at the time and remembers Mary Thomas coming in for her appointments. Ruth recalls:

> It was a nightmare! There was only one thing worse than the fittings. That was when Mrs Thomas would arrive with a suit Bon Marche had made years before, instructing that it was to be unpicked, turned, and made up again on the reverse side. When the head girl tried to explain that there was a 'right' and a 'wrong'side to the fabric, Mrs Thomas simply refused to listen and just started telling me to be careful not to cut the material when I was unpicking it![20]

Hilda Brown of Victoria Park, one of Mrs Boom's daughters, was also a talented seamstress, and was called on when her mother was too busy to sew for Mary. Hilda laughs about the time she was delegated to make a full-length magenta velvet gown.

> The problem was, Mrs Raine wouldn't stand still long enough for me to fit the garment and put pins in place. Her mind was on

> the downstairs lounge and what might be happening there. She fidgeted so much I know I could have got a better fit by just estimating![21]

Mary may not have been over-concerned with fashionable clothes, but she was very particular about her hair and never failed to look well-groomed. When young, Harry Love of City Beach worked for one of Perth's leading hairdressers of the time - Siegrist and Simon. The salon was located in Hay Street, above Caris Bros Jewellers.

> Mr Simon (Haffner) always looked after Mrs Raine himself. She was in good company at the salon. Lady Mitchell, wife of the governor, patronised Siegrist and Simon, and she liked to remind us that we had the privilege of setting the hair of the wife of the first governor of Western Australia. Others who had held what seemed to be the same office had been lieutenant governors.[22]

Mary soon realised that in Mrs Boom she had acquired a dependable deputy who could be trusted to run the house, kitchen and dining room as she would herself. She could turn her attention to other matters knowing that these key areas were in good hands.

One of the duties Mrs Boom took over from Mary was organising functions which were booked from time to time in the dining room, but Mary always planned the menus and gave quotes herself.

Len Brennan of Mt Lawley was so impressed with a dinner he organised at the Wentworth on behalf of The West Australian Newspapers Cricket Club on Saturday 19 March 1938, that he still has the program of the night's events. The menu offered soup, fish, entree, choice of roast meats and vegetables, choice of sweets with cream and ice cream, tea or coffee. There were fifty guests, and the total cost was £10.0.0![23]

In 1938, Mary decided to lease the Bohemia to a partnership formed by two of Perth's leading and most experienced hotel keepers - Alan Shepherd and Gordon Hack. Alan Shepherd was the new licensee, but it was Gordon Hack who consulted with Mary in 1939 on extensive alterations and remodelling work.

Although Mary threw herself into the venture with characteristic optimism, she was fully aware of the ominous rumblings in Europe. Being British by birth, the general sense of disquiet was probably more real to her than to those around her. The average Australian was still able to feel comfortably detached from the threatening events on the other side of the world. After all, Germany, Poland, Czechoslovakia, were a long way from these shores.

Pushing these concerns to the back of her mind, Mary enlisted architect Mr W G Bennett to prepare plans for alterations to the Bohemia Hotel. The changes were designed to elevate the Bohemia to a first class city hotel. Before they were completed Gordon Hack and Alan Shepherd, with Mary's approval, sold their lease to Mr J D (Jack) Healy. Like Gordon Hack, who was described at the time as 'Perth's liveliest hotel keeper', Jack Healy was another colourful personality.

Work at the Bohemia was completed in June 1939. Mary had no way of knowing that in just three months, it would be impossible to call on any resources to carry out hotel alterations.

No further changes were made to the Bohemia Hotel until 1985, twenty five years after Mary's death.

Busy as Mary was upgrading her city hotels, she still found time to look further afield for good business opportunities. She became interested in the Bullsbrook Hotel. It was situated some thirty miles from Perth and, although she had previously restricted her hotel investments to the metropolitan area, she recognised the unique potential of this particular licence.

The original hotel had been built in 1912 for a Mr Reynolds, who became the first licensee. It had replaced two of the very early hotels in the district - Ye Old Bush Inne, some five miles south, and Cockman's Hotel, about two or three miles to the north. The hotel was relatively small, but provided a welcome centre for the local community and a staging post for travellers on the Great Northern Highway and Chittering Road. Towards the end of the 1920s, the Commonwealth Government took over a local landmark known as Woodley Orchard Estate and established the Pearce Air Force Base.

It was a bonus for Bullsbrook because the construction provided work for a lot of local men, carrying through to retirement for many of them.

The base became progressively busier, and increasing numbers of Air Force personnel spent their leisure hours at the hotel. Towards the late 1930s, the then owner, William (Bill) Newton, started work to upgrade the hotel to provide better facilities for the new patrons. Mary negotiated to lease the hotel from him when the work was completed.

About this time a big jovial farmer from Manmanning, in Western Australia's south west district, was becoming a frequent guest at the Wentworth. He signed the hotel register Arnold Yeldham Raine, but introduced himself as Joe.

Chapter 5

It is my melancholy duty to inform you that..............Australia is at war

1939 - 1943

On that fateful day, 3 September 1939, little more than an hour after the British Prime Minister, Neville Chamberlain, declared that Britain was at war with Germany, his Australian counterpart, Robert Menzies, announced on radio that it was his 'melancholy duty to inform Australians that in consequence of a persistence by Germany in her invasion of Poland, Great Britain has declared war upon her and that, as a result, Australia is also at war.'

The impact of Menzies' declaration was not felt immediately in Western Australia. In the early days it was easy to live by the Prime Minister's catch-cry of 'business as usual'.

Once again, it was not a good time to begin a new venture, but Mary was committed to take over the lease of the upgraded Bullsbrook Hotel in January 1940. She renamed it Chequers Hotel, after the country residence of the British Prime Minister and, as she had done with most of her hotel purchases, installed George as licensee. He took over from William (Bill) Newton, who then replaced him at the United Service Hotel. The obvious advantage of having a monopoly to cater for the adjacent Air Force Base had been Mary's prime motive in acquiring the hotel, but she soon discovered that the problems associated with running it far outweighed the financial advantages. [1]

Zoe Garbutt recalls her mother telling her that Mary Thomas, as she was at the time, had difficulty staffing the hotel from the small pool of labour available at Bullsbrook, and when busy nights were anticipated she would pay for a bus to take any of the Wentworth staff who volunteered, to work at the Chequers.[2]

The distance from Perth proved to be an insurmountable obstacle to the efficient supervision of the hotel, and just two years later Mary returned the lease to Bill Newton, whilst he returned his lease of the United Service Hotel to her. It was her only hotel investment outside city limits, and she decided to concentrate her interests where she could keep her finger on the pulse.

Almost immediately, Mary bought a lease of the Newmarket Hotel in Pier Street, just a few city blocks east of the Wentworth. She felt very comfortable with its proximity, and it provided a home and work for several members of her family. As always with new acquisitions, George was the first licensee.

Though the events of the war were taking place a long way from Perth, subtle changes soon became evident. West Australians quickly forgot their earlier attempt to secede from the Commonwealth and became part of a united Australian war effort.

After the Prime Minister's announcement, West Australian men flocked to enlist. The early enthusiasm was kept alive by a compelling Commonwealth recruitment campaign, but as the war situation became increasingly serious, it was evident that all eligible men would eventually be called up. This possibility motivated many to enlist in the service of their choice rather than wait to be drafted.

The departure of enlisted men provided employment opportunities for many who had remained unemployed beyond the aftermath of the Depression. Additional work became available when a large number of defence facilities were constructed in Western Australia and existing local industries converted to wartime production.

With the outbreak of war came the appearance of recruiting offices, air-raid shelters, and centres for war loan appeals and rallies. Community organisations such as the Australian Comforts Fund,

Red Cross, Young Men's Christian Association and Salvation Army, called for volunteers to provide social support for departing and visiting servicemen. There were many other organisations, all of which played an important role during the war years, and their contribution has been well documented.

The internment of residents not of Australian birth, overt racist propaganda and strict censorship, were accepted without question, as being necessary for the defence of the country. An early form of regimentation, previously not known in Australia, saw all citizens issued with identification cards, and ration books to control the purchase of food, clothing and petrol.

Then as always, there were the cheats who evaded any kind of war or defence work, and those who saw the situation as an opportunity to make easy money. Black marketing, hoarding, profiteering and illegal trading in ration coupons were rife.

A concerted campaign encouraged women to volunteer for essential industry, take a factory job, join one of the women's services or the Australian Women's Land Army, to support their fighting men and make a personal contribution to the war effort.

Many women responded to this call and found themselves caught up in an exciting new experience. They soon learned they could hold down jobs previously only available to men. They also discovered, when placed in authority they could get the job done. This confidence, together with the fact that they were earning their own money, gave women a new sense of independence. In the long term, though, it was never going to be easy to overturn centuries of tradition, and when the war ended women were expected to return to their traditional role of wife and mother.

In the early days the term 'phoney war' was bandied about a lot, and even towards the closing months of 1941 Western Australia remained relatively untouched by the conflict. Although there was grief and concern at seeing husbands and sons leave for places unknown, those who stayed behind never considered they too could face the threat of invasion. Then came a series of events which changed forever the notion that Australians, and West Australians with them, would be spared the grimmer aspects of war.

Reality hit home on 19 November 1941 with the incredible news that HMAS *Sydney* had been sunk by the German raider *Kormoran*, a heavily armed, disguised merchant ship. The *Sydney* had been on patrol off the undefended West Australian coast near Carnarvon. The full complement of 645 men was lost with the ship. In the interest of maintaining public morale, reports focused on the capture of 315 survivors from the *Kormoran* rather than on the devastating losses from the *Sydney.*

More disturbing news was quick to follow. On Sunday 7 December 1941, less than three weeks after the sinking of the *Sydney*, Japan launched a surprise air attack on the American base of Pearl Harbour in Hawaii. The attack left 3,435 Americans killed or wounded, stunning the American people out of their reluctance to be drawn into what they considered was a European war.

If Australians had not yet accepted the gravity of the situation, any remaining complacency crumbled as a series of events early in 1942 brought the theatre of war frighteningly close to home.

Morale plummeted when Singapore fell on 15 February. Two days later when a Japanese air raid on Darwin resulted in the death of at least 243 people, invasion appeared imminent. More tragic news followed within weeks. On 1 March of the same year, the light cruiser HMAS *Perth*, named after the Western Australian capital, was sunk by the Japanese fleet in the Sunda Strait. Half of the crew was lost, and most of the survivors were captured by the Japanese. Two days later Broome was bombed by Japanese forces, causing destruction of millions of pounds worth of Allied equipment, including seven American planes and three flying boats as well as thirteen other Australian, British and Dutch aircraft.

The obvious escalation of the war made Australians feel increasingly isolated - an isolation felt even more keenly by West Australians. Common sense warned that if the situation continued to worsen, Britain could not be counted on to defend this outpost of her Empire, and there was a general acceptance of the idea that Australia should look to America to ensure its safety.

When American servicemen began arriving in Perth in February and March 1942 they were welcomed by the local population. Because of strict censorship, no publicity was given to the friendly invasion, but the American presence offered reassurance to a population well aware that most fully trained Australian troops were overseas with the AIF. Only partially trained troops and volunteers remained to defend the country. Rivalries which later surfaced between the Americans and members of the Australian forces were certainly not evident in the early days.

Mary Raine, or 'Ma' Thomas, as she was at the time, was aware of the pending arrival of American submariners some time before it became general knowledge. Early in 1942 she was approached by the Defence Department, acting for the American Consulate, and advised that the Wentworth Hotel would be required by the United States Navy to accommodate submarine crews when they returned to Perth on leave between patrols.[3] This was not a request. It was a requisition. In effect, for the duration of the war Mary would share ownership of the Wentworth. On the ground floor her jurisdiction ceased at the door of the dining room and beyond to the kitchen, where providoring and preparation of meals passed into the hands of US Navy personnel. Though submariners seeking accommodation registered at the reception desk in the usual way, all accommodation was paid by the Navy. The agreed single rate was ten shillings and sixpence per night. Mary continued to run the bars and drinking lounges. A small household consisting of herself, Mrs Boom, Mrs Boom's daughter Roz Dearing, who worked at the hotel, Paddy Baker and a few other permanent guests occupied quarters which were temporarily separated from the main body of the accommodation. They took meals in the dining room per courtesy of the US Navy.[4]

Mary was not particularly pleased about relinquishing any part of her hotel, but when she voiced her reluctance via a direct approach to the Defence Department, the commanding officer looked at her and said: 'Mrs Thomas. Do you realise there's a war on?'[5]

Many of Perth's hotels were similarly requisitioned. Only the Esplanade and Adelphi were considered suitable quarters for commissioned officers. Lower ranks monopolised the city's more modest accommodation, and this included the Wentworth.

Different arms of the American Navy formed their own special allegiances within the nominated group of hotels. For instance, the Catalina crews, Navy flyers stationed at Crawley Bay, known as the 'Airdales', made their social headquarters at the Nedlands Park Hotel, whereas the submariners, or 'Black Shoe' adopted the Wentworth and the Ocean Beach in Cottesloe. There seemed to be mutual suspicion between the two groups and they were at pains to avoid each other. On those occasions when the two arms of the Navy met, it was not unusual for a fight to result. One such incident is recorded in 'Fleeting Attraction', a social history of the time, written by Anthony J Barker and Lisa Jackson.

> Catalina pilot, Bill Barker recalled a major altercation, involving servicemen of several nationalities, in which submariners hurled huge plant pots from the upstairs balcony of the Wentworth Hotel onto opponents in the street below. [6]

Not all the visiting submariners frequented hotels. Many were able to organise the social aspect of their lives within days of arriving. A meeting with local girls saw them welcomed into private homes, where both hosts and guests benefited from the newly-formed friendships. The Americans had access to luxuries denied to the locals, and they became renowned for their generosity.[7]

During the 'occupation' by the American submariners, romance blossomed and many a Perth girl found the man of her dreams. Not all the resulting unions were successful, but then, happy marriage cannot be guaranteed even in less unusual and stressful times.

Kathleen (Kath) Pouleris shared with me memories of meeting her future husband William (Bill), a submariner based at Fremantle.

> Bill was young and a long way from his home. After we met, my family invited him to share meals and outings and to enjoy a taste of Western Australian hospitality Our courtship was very traditional. It survived a two-year separation when Bill's submarine was sent back to the United States for repairs. When he returned to Fremantle, our friendship developed and we became engaged in May 1944.

The US Navy had strict requirements which had to be met by couples wishing to marry. Our wedding day was quite dramatic. We were to be married by special licence on 12 July 1945, but the necessary Permission to Marry document did not arrive until 3.00 p.m. on the day of the big event. The Registry Office stayed open for us until 5.00 p.m. to issue the licence and we were married at 6.00 p.m.

Soon afterwards Bill left on another patrol. We had no way of knowing the end of the war was in sight, but peace was declared just three weeks after he left. Bill went back to the US and I joined him there in June 1946. Bill loved Perth and we returned to make our home here in 1959. Ours was a lasting and happy marriage.[8]

The majority of airmen and submariners relied on the hotels for entertainment and relief from the pressures of combat. The Wentworth earned its popularity by offering music and dancing - an ideal atmosphere in which to meet the young women who flocked there in the hope of catching the eye of a handsome American. Mary was besieged by girls wanting to work as barmaids or stewardesses. She told me: 'They would have happily worked without pay.'[9]

Once Mary accepted that she could no longer accommodate the country visitors who had become the mainstay of the house trade, and the day-to-day catering was out of her hands, it was almost a relief to be able to devote all her energy to supervising the lounge and bars. She was an astute businesswoman and not slow to realise that this unexpected set of circumstances would enable her to make substantially increased profits.

Only US Navy personnel were permitted in the residential section of the hotel. Women were not allowed upstairs.[10] That is not to say the men didn't manage to break the rules at times. Rumours persist to this day that women were regularly smuggled upstairs by the Americans. It was wartime, and it would be naive to suggest that this never happened at the Wentworth, or any other hotel for that matter, however, where the rumours go further and suggest that Mary Raine abetted these activities and profited from them, a biographer has an obligation to probe those possibilities.

Painstaking research of Police, Liquor Licensing and Defence records failed to uncover any recorded evidence of relevant charges having been brought against Mary Raine. Despite this lack of documentary evidence and adamant denials from those who are qualified to remember the Wentworth during the war years, hearsay persists that it was a hotel 'of a certain reputation' - the words of the late Perth City Councillor, Rod Evans. There is no foundation in fact to support that description, and I do not propose to perpetuate an urban myth. A nudge and a wink do not present a very compelling argument. So why do the rumours continue to haunt her memory?

Mary Raine was unique in that she became wealthy through her own financial acumen and hard work, in an era when a woman who acquired riches usually did so by sharing her husband's success, or through inheritance. Mary's obvious wealth attracted public attention and a degree of notoriety, and the suggested link with prostitution was an easy way to explain away her extraordinary financial achievements.

From the time the re-built Wentworth was opened in 1928 until 1952, twelve minor charges were listed against the licence. These covered serving liquor on Sunday, serving in areas other than those designated by the licence, serving under-age patrons, allowing betting on licensed premises, and fictitious description of liquor[11] - a roundabout way of stating that water had been added to liquor for bar sales.

When interviewed, ex-servicemen recalled that the Wentworth lounge could be counted on as a place to meet a partner for the evening, but if something more than sharing a drink was planned they had to find somewhere else to go.[12]

Francis ('Gunner') Signore of Fallon, Nevada, USA, was a submariner who served on the USS *Raton* and USS *Blackfin* operating out of Fremantle between 1942 and 1945. He remembers the Wentworth well, having stayed there for two weeks in January 1944 and again for the same length of time in December of that year.

> My impression of the Wentworth Hotel was that it was mighty fine - a little old but always neat and clean. Service was one

> hundred per cent and the Navy food was excellent, three times a day with seconds and thirds if you wanted it. Girls were not allowed in the rooms but welcomed at the bar and on the dance floor.
> Perth impressed me as a clean friendly city. No trash or litter lying around. I remember the taxis with the charcoal burner mounted on the rear bumper, replacing gasoline because there wasn't any. Going up-hill was a problem. Us sailors would have to get out and push - not easy when we were roaring with laughter and our girl friends trying to pull us back inside the taxi.
> Perth weather was great. We wore white uniforms in summer, blues when it got a little cooler.
> Perth girls were number one in my book - always cheerful and lively, and dressed well, considering there wasn't much money floating around. They really loved to dance and we were more than eager to partner them.
> The hospitality of West Australians was outstanding. We were strangers in their country but we were treated with affection and respect. We understood that food, especially meat, was limited to what could be obtained through ration coupons, yet we were invited to our girlfriends' homes and enjoyed some wonderful meals. Sometimes we were able to help out with coffee, chocolate, cigarettes and liquor.
> Prostitutes did not frequent the Wentworth or Ocean Beach Hotels where we spent most of our shore leave. It was no use trying to sneak girls in - the hotels had forbidden it. However, the existence of Roe (I think that is how you spell it) Street, was common knowledge and I remember there were some lovely ladies at that address!
> I still have the very fondest memories of those days spent in Perth during 1943, 1944 and 1945, and have retained valued friendships made during those times.[13]

Robert Goodhart of Pottstown, Pensylvania, USA, remembers his wartime leave spent at the Wentworth. In response to an appeal for information which was published on my behalf in *Polaris*, the official organ of retired submariners in the US, he has sent me this memoir.

> I am 78 years old, but I remember Ma Thomas well. I served aboard the USS *Hake* (SS-256) and stayed at the Wentworth Hotel at least three times. It was a great place to recuperate after a war patrol.

> Ma Thomas was a kind and cheerful person, and never got angry at our wild escapades. I met her during my first stay at the hotel. As I carried my seabag up the head of the stairs, she was standing there and asked me for my money. She took my two months' pay and locked it in her safe after giving me £20 to spend. She told me to come and get more money when that ran out. She was afraid I would spend it or lose it all at once. She was a very thoughtful person. Some of the things you have heard about what went on at the Wentworth are probably true and there's a lot more you haven't heard about, but that had nothing to do with Ma Thomas.
>
> I really loved Australia. I belong to the Subvets of WWII and on my reunion vest I proudly display the Australian flag, as we subvets who operated from Fremantle consider Australia our second country and we all like the Aussies.[14]

Len Brennan of Mt Lawley remembers that in the early years of the war, before the Wentworth Hotel was requisitioned by the US Navy, a serviceman and his girlfriend could book a room if he was clever enough to get past the receptionist. Len recalled an occasion when a couple he knew told him about their rendezvous at the Wentworth. However, he totally dismissed any suggestion that girls could be procured at the hotel. 'Absolutely not', said Len. 'The servicemen had to do their own hunting'.[15]

Dr Carl Georgeff, Mary's friend and medical practitioner, deplored the fact that rumours bred in wartime could possibly be given credibility today.

> There is no truth whatsoever in suggestions that Mary Raine was involved in any aspect of prostitution. In wartime you can't stop servicemen from sneaking women up the back stairs. It should be remembered that the US Navy requisitioned the residential section of the Wentworth, and what happened there was almost beyond Mary Raine's control after 1942. She couldn't guard the stairs twenty four hours a day. As her physician as well as her friend, I do know that she was mortified when the rumours reached her, especially when it was touted to be part of the reason a ban was placed on the hotel by the Australian Military authorities. Mary made a direct approach to the Prime Minister, West Australian John Curtin, and the ban was removed within days. I hardly think the Prime Minister would have allowed

himself to become personally involved if there was the slightest substance to the rumours.[16]

During the war years when the American presence was most evident in Perth, Harry Murray of East Cannington was a young man working at Brear and Doonan, next to the Bohemia Hotel in Murray Street. He remembers the chatter in the lunch room.

> The older men would be talking about the Wentworth, laughing and joking as they described Mary Raine standing at the top of the stair landing, stopping the Yanks from getting their girlfriends upstairs. The hotel was a bit notorious in those days because it was so busy, and there seemed to be a lot of fighting between our servicemen and the Americans on the street outside. My sister worked opposite the Wentworth and remembers when an Australian soldier rode into the foyer of the hotel on horseback![17]

Morgan Smith of Australind recalls visiting the Wentworth with his father, who had served in the RAAF. It was soon after the end of the war, and the purpose of the visit was to talk about old times with Mary Raine, whom his father had known as Mary Thomas, when she ran a boarding house in Mornington Mills back around 1909.

> I was a very young man at the time, but I remember the conversation as though it was yesterday. I probably pricked up my ears because the discussion was about the rumours that had attached to the hotel about the goings-on of the American submariners when they stayed there during the war. Mary Raine agreed that at times the men managed to elude her guard. According to her, the US Navy did not encourage the behaviour, but could have done more to stop it happening.[18]

I asked Roz Dearing for her comments on a quote from 'Fleeting Attraction', the work of authors Anthony J Barker and Lisa Jackson.

> The Yanks would take their girls to hotels such as the Wentworth where 'old Ma Thomas was robbing them every way but getting away with it - they didn't care.' They would spend the night there 'and then of course our boys would wait for the Yanks and belt them up.'[19]

The authors were quoting Mrs Pat White, 'a teenager at the start of the war'. Roz was outraged.

> That is nonsense. Where do people get this sort of information? I lived at the Wentworth during the war years and would like to

> speak to those who consider they know more about what happened at the hotel than I do. The office was next to the lift and the foot of the stairs. Mrs Raine would be out of the office in a flash when she heard people going upstairs, checking that they were bona fide guests. I'm not saying that the Yanks never succeeded in getting past her guard - it would be ridiculous to suggest that - but to imply that Mrs Raine encouraged that sort of behaviour and made money out of it is preposterous.[20]

It has been brought to my attention that 'according to popular legend in Perth, Mary Raine made the bulk of her fortune by making rooms available at the Wentworth to American servicemen for casual liaisons and charging very high rates for the privilege'. The legend is not supported by fact. The Wentworth, Bohemia, United Service and Windsor Hotels, which represented the bulk of Mary Raine's fortune were all bought before 1930. Where mortgages still remained on those properties, the title deeds do not record any having been discharged via an unusual influx of funds between 1942 and 1944.

The Mary Raine I knew was a stickler for morality. She was almost paranoid about checking that couples claiming to be married, were married, before they could book into her hotel - no luggage, no room! Her rules were ably enforced by Mrs Boom and receptionist Mrs Isgar, who shared their employer's moral code. In those years the Licensing Act contained a rather archaic and ambiguous law forbidding licensed premises 'being used as a house of ill-fame' - a euphemism for allowing prostitution. A conviction on those grounds resulted in the loss of the Publican's General Licence.

The civilian population may have taken the Americans to its heart, but as time went by Australian servicemen became increasingly resentful of the glamorous visitors, and when they met there was little semblance of friendship.

For Mary, as a hotelkeeper, this situation was not helped when Western Command banned the sale of bottled beer to Australian men in uniform. In mid 1942, the Swan Brewery was ordered to cut production by a third, in order to release some of its labour force for war work.[21] This led to the rationing of supplies to hotels.

Anthony J Barker and Lisa Jackson, authors of 'Fleeting Attraction' comment on this development.

> While Australians chafed under such restrictions, American servicemen could obtain signed vouchers from their officers, to purchase beer direct from the Swan Brewery.[22]
> Naturally, alcohol was not only symbolic of often resented American affluence but also a fuel for violence. The Australian Department of Information distributed a brochure to United States troops soon after they arrived warning them of the dangers of Australian alcohol: 'Australians drink considerable quantities of beer - watch your step with it - it is a whole lot heavier and more alcoholic than most United States beers. Australian wines also have to be watched. The cheapest grades have a kick like T.N.T.' It might have added that so did Australian troops when filled with either wine or beer.[23]

Mary lost no time in putting the Wentworth on a wartime footing. A four-piece jazz band played daily from 3.00 p.m. until closing time at 6.00 p.m. On Friday evenings the hotel foyer was cleared to allow dancing on its polished tiled surface. Mary believed thirsty customers should not be kept waiting, so there was never a shortage of staff, and girls were eager for the work, seeing a chance to meet an American and earn the generous tips for which they became legendary.

On the side wall of the lounge, close by the bar door from which the stewardesses - drink waiters as they are now called - emerged with laden trays, was a high jarrah desk. It looked rather like a pulpit, delivered to the wrong address! It accommodated a cash register and a high stool from which Mary could watch what was going on even in the farthest corners of the room. Each stewardess was issued with a £10.0.0 float. She paid at the desk for her tray of drinks before delivering them to her tables. It was an efficient way of ensuring that no drinks were given away, and there was no possibility of tips being confused with what rightly belonged in the till. Mary could run her eye over a full tray of assorted drinks and state its value in less time than it would take today's shop assistant to punch the first amount into the calculator. The supervision also made sure that customers did not wait for service.

The desk was Mary's special domain and only exceptional circumstances prevented her from taking up her position there between 3.00 p.m. and 6.00 p.m. every trading day. The war had ended before hotel closing time advanced to 9.00 p.m. in 1946, Western Australia being one of the first States to adopt extended liquor licensing hours. It was a very civilised step towards abolishing the 'six o'clock swill' - the popular term to describe the last minute panic to get extra drinks before the bar closed, a demeaning aspect of drinking in all States.

The Wentworth lounge became extremely popular with the US submariners. They appreciated the music and dancing but couldn't understand why everything ground to a halt at 6.00 p.m. Unless there was prior knowledge of where the police would be turning a blind eye on a particular night, the evening was over. The Americans found it all rather baffling, but are reported to have found their own solution by hiding caches of liquor under their bunks.

At most times the atmosphere at the Wentworth was happy and relaxed. The guests, returned safely from war patrol, had two weeks in which to unwind, have fun and put the horrors of the conflict behind them.

Roz Dearing remembers vividly those occasions when the atmosphere was not happy or relaxed - the times when there was news of losses at sea.

> When a submarine was due to return to Fremantle from a patrol, there'd be a great flurry of activity, especially around the kitchens. This information was censored, but when you lived on the premises it was impossible not to be aware of what was going on. Sometimes, not often thank God, everything suddenly went very quiet. The noise in the kitchen and dining room stopped, and you knew there'd be no howls of laughter and yelling for food that night.[24]

Nineteen forty-three was a difficult year. It was inevitable that unpleasantness between Australian and US servicemen surfaced from time to time, and on occasion these altercations spilt into the Wentworth even if they had started on the streets outside. No reports of this type of feuding appeared in the newspapers. Censorship ensured that readers were not confronted with news items reporting the allies warring among themselves. There was an unusually high incidence of these fights early in 1943 - all of them beyond Mary's control. Reminiscing about those times she recalled her consternation when the Australian Army placed a ban on her hotel.

> One night a soldier called at the Wentworth. He saluted and handed me a document. It was a notice that the hotel had been placed out of bounds to Australian troops.
> The Army refused to give a reason for the ban - they said they didn't have to give reasons.
> We wrote to our West Australian Prime Minister, John Curtin, and to Senator Dorothy Tangney , asking them to do something about the ban. I always believed in going straight to the top.
> The ban on the Wentworth was lifted after about a week. I think it must have been a mistake.[25]

Mistake or not, Mary was distressed by the incident. At such times she realised she was very much alone, and thought how comforting it would be to have a partner to share the load.

The year did not get better. In November, the hotel licence came up for review and contrary to expectation, was not renewed automatically. The Chairman of the Licensing Court was critical of the fact that the management had permitted alcohol to be consumed in areas other than those designated for the purpose. His comment referred directly to the hotel entrance and foyer where dancing was held on Friday nights and where over-flow lounge customers were seated every evening. In addition, the toilet facilities had come in for unfavourable mention. The licence was renewed for only three months, subject to immediate attention to these shortcomings.[26]

The derogatory comments caused Mary considerable distress. Anyone who has held a hotel licence knows that directions from the Licensing Court cannot be dismissed or taken lightly. Dancing in the foyer stopped immediately and work started on a new toilet block.

It was a relief for Mary to discuss her problems with the friendly farmer from Manmanning. His visits were becoming more frequent and she found herself looking forward to them. Though she now had only limited access to the hotel accommodation, she made sure there was always a room for Joe Raine.

Chapter 6

'Rainee'

1890 - 1943

Arnold Yeldham Raine was born in Victoria in 1890. At the time of his birth his father was 22, his mother 41.

Eileen Timewell of Kalamunda provides the basis for the following history.

The Arnold Raine story had its beginnings in Oxfordshire, England, in the village of Burdrop, near Banbury.

This picturesque village was the birthplace of James Manning who was born there on 17 August 1814. A dedicated scholar, James completed his studies to begin a successful supervisory career. In this capacity he took over responsibility for several London houses, notably those of the Duke of Cleveland, Lord Ashburton, Lord Baybrook and Lord Kilmoy.

His success brought him to the attention of Captain Henderson, who selected James to join him on the ship *Scandian*, bound for special service in Western Australia. The ship arrived in Fremantle in 1850. James was accompanied by his wife and two small children, James and Jane, along with seventy-five convicts, the first of the 9,636 prisoners that were eventually sent to Western Australia. A third child, Emily, was born in 1853.

James Manning led a succesful life in Perth, and was responsible for the building supervision of many of the State's landmarks. He died in 1893, his wife having predeceased him in 1877.[1]

Their daughter Jane was very artistic and loved music and painting. She was also deeply religious, and with her parents attended St John's Wesleyan Church in Fremantle. Jane worked tirelessly for the church, playing the organ, teaching Sunday School and visiting the sick and underprivileged of the Parish. The death of her mother was a great loss to her. She remained to care for her father long after girls of her era would have married and left home. At the age of thirty-eight she met her future husband, nineteen year old William Raine, at the church they both attended.[2]

William, a carpenter by trade, found it difficult to find regular employment. Soon after the wedding he decided to try his luck in Victoria, and moved there with his wife in late 1887. A daughter was born the following year, but her premature death at the age of three months was a shattering loss, as the couple feared that because of Jane's age there might not be other children. Their concerns were needless. In 1890, with great joy, they welcomed their son, Arnold Yeldham Raine.[3]

Early in the new century, William brought his family back to Perth. They moved into No 5 Waylen Street, Guildford, and William set about establishing himself as a self-employed carpenter. Arnold, who had come to be called 'Joe' by family and friends, was thirteen when enrolled as a day-boy at Guildford Grammar School, and there he completed the early years of his secondary education.[4]

Records made available through courtesy of Rosemary Waller, Guildford Grammar School Archivist, show that Joe Raine was a good scholar, winning prizes in both Arithmetic and Chemistry in his final year. Tall for his age, and well-built, he enjoyed sports and was a 'natural' for the School Rugby Team, holding a place in the 1st XV111 in 1904 and 1905.[5]

The death of Joe's mother Jane, in 1906 came as a crushing blow. He lost interest in completing his final years of secondary education, opting to strike out and look for work. He tried his hand at a variety of jobs and for a brief time was employed in the advertising section at the offices of *The Daily News*. However, Joe loved to be out of doors and began to think seriously of putting city life behind him and trying his luck in the pearling industry in Broome.

Courtesy Guildford Grammar Archives

Joe Raine - Guildford Rugby Team 1904 - centre, back row

When his father William, told him of his intention to remarry, Joe felt that the decision to leave home had been made for him. In 1913 William Raine married a forty-two year old widow from the Guildford area - Mary Amelia Skoglund. They lived in the Waylen Street house, Mary continuing her career and becoming well known as the district nurse. When both retired in 1928, they moved to 68 Swan Street Guildford. However, William was not ready for a life of complete leisure and he decided to avail himself of what was known as the Group Settlement Scheme and take up a lease of grazing land in the Manmanning area. In the light of subsequent events this may have been to pave the way for his son Joe, to take over, should he ever decide to turn his hand to farming. William divided his time between the property and the home in Guildford until Mary's death on 16 November 1936, followed soon after by his own death on 12 October 1937.

Joe arrived in Broome during 1914, ready to try his luck in an industry he knew little about.

At the turn of the century, Broome could have been described as the pearling capital of the world, with eighty per cent of all pearl shell originating from there. Nevertheless, there had been a significant downturn in the industry, the number of pearling ship licences falling from a peak of 413 in 1907 to just 193, a statistic which would be expected to deter a newcomer. However, Joe saw this as a challenge, as well as an opportunity to acquire a ship at a good price. He spent the first six months learning about the industry, making contacts and tracking down a dependable vessel.

Val Burton, President of the Broome Historical Society, provided the basis for the following information.

> During the fourteen years Joe spent in Broome, he was master of three pearling luggers. The first, *Llyris* was licensed to him in 1915. It was a two-masted schooner, almost 17 tons, dimensions 40.25 x 15.75 x 8.9 feet, built at Fremantle by Edward Howson for Charles Henry Blackman in 1914. Available records do not show whether Joe bought this ship outright or operated it in partnership with Charles Blackman. Joe was certainly the licensee and he retained the *Llyris* throughout his stay in the

industry. The *Australind* was acquired in 1917 but relinquished the following year. In 1921 *La Perouse*, an older smaller lugger was licensed to him. Built in 1910, a two-masted schooner, 13.43 tons, dimensions 40.2 x 14 x 4.75 feet, it had been built in Fremantle by A E Brown for George Moss. Joe retained this ship also, until 1927.[6]

Joe was relatively successful and he remained in Broome for thirteen years - but it is doubtful if he could have started in the industry at a less auspicious time. A succession of bad seasons resulted in traditional buyers looking to other markets for pearl shell. Pearlers might dream of finding the glowing gem that would bring them wealth, but the life-blood of the industry was in finding and selling pearl shell.

When Joe decided to try his luck, trading was at a very low ebb. The government of the day recognised that the fledgling pearl shell industry was in trouble and offered an advance of £100 per ton to the pearlers. They were in the unhappy situation of having to refuse it, as they were in debt to creditors, who had first option to purchase. The refusal meant that the matter was shelved and the situation simply got worse.

Before the war, shell had been auctioned at the Bull Wharf in London, and from 1919 to 1926 was sold through brokers in New York. In 1927, Broome pearlers themselves negotiated an agreement to sell to a sole distributor, the Otto Gerdau Company of New York, at £180 per ton.

The new agreement was important to the industry and promised to ensure viability for many of the pearlers who had hung on through the bad times. It came into force the year Joe left Broome and returned to Perth. He had had enough. He surrendered his licences in 1927.

The tides of time have washed away all but brief glimpses of the thirteen years Joe spent in Broome. A photograph (undated), made available by the Broome Historical Society, shows a good looking young man, lithe and fit, wavy brown hair neatly styled, nibbling the end of his pencil, a habit that stayed with him. Twenty-five years later, it would be rare to broach him in his office and not find him doing exactly that.

The following excerpt from the *Nor West Echo*, dated 25 July 1925, describes an episode which was typical of the era and the industry.

> On Tuesday night Mr A Y Raine's auxiliary lugger *Llyris* nearly came to grief on the east side of the jetty. The crew had anchored close to the jetty, for the purpose of filling up with water from the pipes, but, during the night a strong wind blew up, and the vessel dragged her anchor. The crew became excited and, had it not been for the owner's timely arrival on the scene, there would have been an accident. As it was, however, Mr Raine got up a sail and took the vessel out of danger.[7]

Whilst in Broome, Joe shared a pearlers' cottage with Charles ('Charlie') Blackman. The type of cottages favoured by pearlers well before the turn of the century are still being built today. The style has endured because it is completely in tune with the climate and environment. Built on short stilts to allow free passage of air beneath the building, Joe's cottage comprised two bedrooms, generous living and working area, bathroom and kitchen; almost a perfect square surrounded on all sides by wide verandahs. These were enclosed by open rails to within half a metre of the ground where slotted 'wings' opened to capture prevailing breezes. This description would fit perfectly the cottages occupied today by visitors to Broome's Cable Beach Resort, but without their modern conveniences.

The cottage Joe shared with Charles Blackman was one of a row situated opposite the Continental Hotel on the Bay side, with nothing to disturb the view of blue water and bluer skies. The hotel, now renamed the Mercure Continental, is still very much a part of Broome life, but the original pearlers' cottages have been demolished to make way for open parklands.

Joe was 37 when he returned to Perth. He had no special plans. His father, who had recently taken up the grazing lease on land in Manmanning, sold him on the idea of turning his energies to farming.[8]

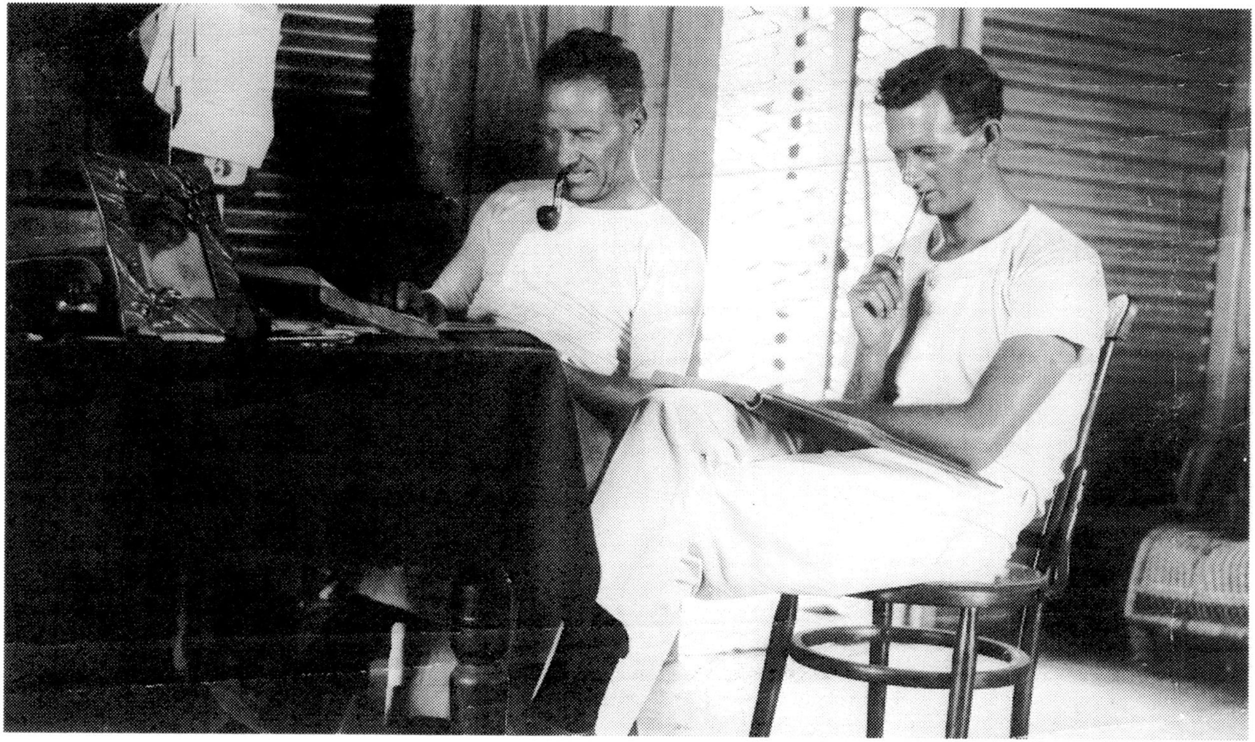

Courtesy Broome Historical Society

Joe Raine (right) taken in pearler's cottage he shared with 'Charlie' Brockman - circa 1920

'Two blocks adjoining mine are available. We could combine the three and have a good selection. Once you get settled, and decide if you like the life, I'll transfer mine to you. The terms are dead easy. You pay little more than £1.0.0 annually for the first five years. In that time you have to complete a certain amount of fencing, clearing and planting, but the Department doesn't expect too much.'

'Slow down,' Joe broke in.

'No. Hear me out. After five years they ask you to pay about £20 a year, and you can work the land on that basis for 20 years, or you can buy it outright for four shillings and sixpence an acre. There's no easier way to set yourself up on your own property. Mind you, you'll have to work.'

Joe had nothing to lose. He travelled south and found no difficulty in arranging a lease. The previous lessee had walked off the farm he acquired. This was not unusual, despite the easy terms offered by the Crown Lands Department. The property was in the Manmanning district between Koorda and Wongan Hills. When combined with the land William had secured earlier, it formed an L-shaped property of just under 3,000 acres, bounded by Koorda Road to the north, Manmanning Road, south, Salvare Road, west, and Jones Road, east. The road which runs across the area from Jones Road to Salvare Road is today named Raine Road.[9] The total yearly rental on the properties was £5.7.0 for the first five years of the lease, increasing to £45.19.0 for the remaining 20 years. After the burden of overheads in the pearling industry, Joe was more than satisfied with the deal.

John Friend of Bayswater, whose father was farming in the Manmanning district some five to six miles from Joe's property, recalls that it was a poor farm. 'Bad land, bad country - not capable of producing wheat without the kind of fertilisers that became available many years later.'[10]

Although John Friend was a boy at the time, he recalls that the locals considered Joe to be unsuited to farming.

> He was not a hard worker - more like a hard drinker. There were times when he would spend all day in the pub at Wongan Hills. On one occasion, after an exceptionally long session, he came out of the bar and drove the nineteen miles home in the wrong vehicle. Those were the days when the car keys were left in the ignition for safe keeping![11]

John Friend remembers another incident when Joe was driving back to his farm at midnight after a long session spent in the same pub. He drove his truck into a creek-bed filled with the run-off from recent rains. It was near the Friend farm and Joe wakened the family at that ungodly hour demanding to be pulled out. John was sent to harness the horses and play the Good Samaritan.[12]

No form of residence had ever been built on the land Joe acquired, and he set up a typical bachelor's camp, or to be more accurate, a primitive humpy. It was to be purely temporary, but as often happens in such cases, he kept putting off the need to build something more substantial. It may have been a blessing in disguise when he returned from a prolonged visit to Wongan Hills to find the humpy a smouldering ruin. Joe contacted his father and asked him to give a hand with building a proper home. It was early in the 1930s. William had retired and was more than pleased to make himself useful doing something for which he was well qualified.

Together Joe and William built a house that has stood the test of time. Two bedrooms, living room, dining room and large country kitchen. The bathroom shared one end of the generous verandah which surrounded the building, and the laundry was accommodated in a shed detached from the main structure.

The building has been added to over the years - one owner had five daughters - but the essence of the original home remains, and is lived in today. It was one of the first houses of any substance to be completed in the district. The present occupant confirmed that it withstood the effects of the Meckering earthquake of 1968 without the hint of a single crack.[13]

Having no plans to establish a garden, Joe planted a stand of pepper trees. They thrive in poor soil and need little water. Over the years these have taken on a life of their own and now loom above the house, their leaf-laden boughs providing shade and obscurity and their spicy perfume filling the air.

After the house was completed, William continued to make regular visits. Fred Jones, a farmer from Manmanning, was a youngster when his father worked the same property at the time Joe Raine owned a nearby farm. He remembers William pottering about and doing the odd maintenance jobs for a number of years until his death in 1937. Basically, Joe lived on his own. Locals recall he was a 'loner - a man who kept to himself and was difficult to get to know.'[14] This description is completely at odds with the outgoing, friendly host of the Wentworth who I came to know years later.

In the late 1930s, Joe conducted a rather public affair with a married lady of the district. It ended abruptly when her husband learned of the matter![15]

Joe soon realised that wheat growing alone would not provide a viable income, and he entered into an arrangement for a neighbour to crop the property, turning his own attention to pig farming. Others in the area had already entered the field and found it a lucrative alternative to cropping. There was an assured market and the animals were cheap to feed and easy to care for. Joe started with twenty porkers and gradually built up the stock until the numbers exceeded 300.[16]

When he needed a break from the monotony of country life, Joe took off for Perth. On these jaunts he liked to stay in the heart of the city and had initially selected the Wentworth Hotel because it offered offstreet parking for his truck. In time it became a home away from home and he would not think of staying anywhere else. Why would he? Ma Thomas made him very welcome - indeed, he came to be treated like one of the family.

Joe could count on Mrs Boom's daughters, Ethyl and Roz, who were living at the Wentworth at the time, to accompany him to the trots at Gloucester Park on Friday evenings, or even go to the pictures with him. Best of all were the quiet hours after closing when Ma would relax over a beer with house guests and family. At these times, which she seemed to enjoy as much as anyone else, she would unwind, and share her lively opinions on everything under the sun. There was plenty to discuss once war broke out in 1939, bringing with it all manner of changes in everyday life.

Early in 1942, Mary Thomas kept her silence on the pending arrival of the US Naval personnel, due to take over most of the accommodation at the hotel. Joe was as surprised as the rest of the household when this happened, but pleased to learn that he had been nominated with a small number of 'permanent guests', and could continue to come and go as usual, secure in the knowledge that there would be a room for him.

Paddy (Clarence Patrick) Baker was one of those who lived permanently at the Wentworth. He was a bachelor. His occupation of travelling picture-show man would not have appealed to many potential partners, and he seemed to enjoy his solitary existence.

Each month, Paddy took the latest movies to towns throughout the State. These were the days when small country towns did not enjoy the luxury of theatres or drive-ins, and Paddy's arrival at the designated time each month was a significant event. He was a small man, lean and wiry. He needed to be fit to manoeuvre the heavy equipment necessary to set up the show in each of his ports of call.

In time Paddy built drive-in theatres throughout the country areas of the State - fourteen in all - and became the proud owner of the Regal Theatre in Subiaco. Paddy secured his own special place in the history of the suburb and the State, when he left his estate to fund the establishment of The Baker Theatre Trust. The Regal has become a focal point for entertainment in Subiaco.

When in the city between country trips, Paddy made the Wentworth his headquarters; he was a trusted member of the household and regularly joined the after-hours discussions with Mary and Joe.

An unlikely friendship developed between the two men - unlikely, because Joe considered having a drink to be part of living, whereas Paddy was an avowed teetotaller. His father had died when Paddy was a child, as the result of alcohol addiction, and nothing could coax Paddy to take the smallest sip.[17] This certainly did not prevent him enjoying the company of those who did enjoy a drink. Sporting his trademark bow tie, bright shirts, smart trousers and blazers, he was more often than not, the life of the party.

Paddy enjoyed the confidences of both Mary and Joe. Mary, obviously, was a very eligible widow. Although she was unpretentious about her success, it had not gone unnoticed and the extent of her wealth was common knowledge. Consequently she suffered the attentions of a number of unwanted suitors.

Throughout 1942 she was pursued assiduously by one in particular. Paddy took it upon himself to make some discreet inquiries and discovered that the party in question was not only married, but was the father of five children![18] Goodness knows what he had planned to do with those had he finally persuaded Mary to say 'Yes'. Without doubt, Mary was hoping to find the right partner. The burden of running a large and busy hotel under wartime conditions, without support and companionship, was at times almost too much for her. Also, as she confided to Paddy, she needed to marry to get some relief from ever-increasing taxation demands.[19]

Paddy decided that he should play Cupid and revelled in his role of matchmaker. He suggested to Mary that 'the friendly farmer from Manmanning' was interested in developing a closer friendship with her, and then suggested to Joe that Mary would welcome his attentions.[20] Paddy must have been sending messages they both wanted to hear because, incredibly, this outdated approach actually worked.

It was not a time for long discussions over candle-lit dinners. The relationship between Mary and Joe could best be described as a case of two friends quietly coming to the realisation that they could complement each other's life, and that they would be happier together than apart.

During a visit in late November 1943, Joe had supported Mary through the anxiety of the ban placed on the hotel and the upsetting observations made by the chairman of the Licensing Court. Moreover, she had just recovered from one of the debilitating bouts of pneumonia that plagued her regularly and never failed to find her out if she had been under extra stress.

One night, Mary was unusually quiet as she tidied the lounge and checked tills at the end of the day's trading. Joe decided to take the initiative. 'For goodness sake, come out of the place for a while Mary. Get someone else to do this. Let's go to the pictures.'[21]

They didn't have to go far, just down William Street to the Metro Theatre where Clarke Gable and Lana Turner were starring in 'Somewhere I'll Find You'. Perhaps the title was significant. Joe proposed that evening.

Mary had been a widow for twenty-five years; it was Joe's first venture into matrimony. Cynics who saw the marriage as a business arrangement would probably have been surprised to observe the measure of warmth and true affection between them. Mary always called Joe, 'Rainee', except on those rare occasions when they had a difference of opinion, when for a brief time he would become 'Joe'. After their marriage, Joe too used the same pet name for his wife - 'Rainee'. The term was very personal and never used by anyone else.

Chapter 7

We were two pals

1943-1948

Joe and Mary secured a special license and were married ten days later, on Friday 3 December 1943, in the Presbyterian Church in Pier Street. It was a source of amusement to both of them that the presiding minister was a well-known temperance advocate.[1]

The event was reported in *The Daily News* on the day of the wedding.

WENTWORTH LICENSEE WED

> Licensee Mrs M. B. Thomas of the Wentworth Hotel will be married late this afternoon to Manmanning Farmer Arnold Yeldham Raine.
> Rev. G. Tulloch will officiate at the marriage, which is to be at the Presbyterian Church, Pier Street, Perth.
> Said the bride-to-be. 'I am confident that we are going to be happy. We are about the same age, have known each other for a long time. We didn't announce any engagement officially, but we have had an understanding between ourselves.'
> The couple are postponing the honeymoon 'until times are better'.
> They will live at the Wentworth Hotel.
> Tall, grey-haired Mrs Thomas will wear a blue crepe street length frock and matching hat for the wedding. A few friends will be entertained at an informal reception afterwards. Her first husband was killed in an accident 20 years ago.

The marriage was witnessed by Arthur Boyd Smith, US Airforce Officer flying Catalinas, who was a friend of Roz Boom (later Dearing). Mary was sixty-six at the time, Joe was fifty-three. It is interesting to note that Mary's age on the Certificate of Marriage is shown as fifty-six, Joe's as fifty-four, whether by error or design, is a matter for conjecture.

Paddy Baker was very proud of the part he played in paving the way for what was to be a happy and successful union. Years later Mary described Joe as 'a loyal and devoted pal', and told me on many occasions that her years of marriage to him were the happiest of her life. She also said. 'We have never for a moment regretted our decision to marry.'[2] Sixteen years later Paddy Baker was again influential in helping Mary make an important decision - one that would benefit thousands of West Australians and ensure that her name and Joe's would live on and become part of the history of this State.

The announcement of wedding plans came as a surprise to those closest to Mary - all except Paddy - and the news was greeted with a measure of dismay by some of Mary's closer family members. What was Birdie thinking of? Who was this man? Where did he come from? The early incredulity later translated into open objection and hostility.

It is certain Mary never confided in family or staff when she considered marriage with Joe Raine. A trusted retainer like Mrs Boom was as surprised as everyone else, and Mary's sister, Toby, who lived at the Wentworth, had no advance knowledge.

Mary handled her marriage to Joe exactly as she handled her innumerable financial dealings. Paddy Baker always declared that marrying Joe was one of Mary's best ever business deals![3] There is no doubt she thought the merger through very carefully. Fred Jones, whose father farmed the property next to Joe's at Manmanning, remembers Joe telling them he had asked Ma Thomas for a loan of £10.0.0 and she had refused. Just weeks later they were astonished to learn he had married the lady![4] The anecdote is not surprising. Mary had probably already decided she would marry Joe, and thought a loan, however small, could be an embarrassment.

Mary did not consult anyone about the step she planned to take because she had learned to trust her instincts. Moreover, she was

Courtesy The Raine Foundation

Mary and Joe - at time of marriage 1943

fully aware that in choosing a husband she was also choosing a business partner. If she didn't need a second opinion before buying a hotel she certainly didn't need one before accepting a proposal of marriage!

Time proved Mary had made a wise choice.

It was inevitable that Joe would be perceived to be a successful fortune hunter - especially by Mary's relations. It is certainly true that Joe Raine had a good deal to gain from marrying Mary Thomas; security, wealth, status and a wonderful companion. However, Mary herself gained enormously from the marriage. Joe was a man of considerable presence - more than six feet in height and weighing over fifteen stone. He was a bachelor, without family ties. He was well-educated, well-spoken, devoted to his wife, and totally committed to supporting her in everything she did. On the business side, he was the perfect 'mine host'; affable, quick to make friends and popular with both staff and customers.

The early days of the marriage were busy. If Joe thought his frequent visits to the Wentworth had given him an insight into the workings of hotel life he soon discovered he knew virtually nothing. Mary's workload amazed him. It became obvious he could help her significantly by taking over some of the burden, and running the liquor side of the business.

There was a lot to learn and Joe was an apt pupil. Mary taught him hotel management from the ground up, the 'ground' being the cellar which housed the kilderkins of beer, the engine-room of bar trade in those days. Suddenly his life had a focus and purpose that had been missing, and he revelled in the transition from the boredom and isolation of pig-farming to the challenge of sharing Mary's world. Under her expert guidance, he quickly familiarised himself with his duties, ordering the beer, wine and spirits; organising bar staff, preparing rosters, taking stock and checking the percentages every Sunday morning. In time he also took over the daily banking. Joe felt a sense of achievement in being able to relieve his wife of these demanding areas of the hotel work.

Courtesy The Raine Foundation

Joe Raine at the time of his marriage to Mary - 1943

Life at the Wentworth was not all routine. The Windsor and United Service Hotels were under management and Joe and Mary visited these at least once a month to discuss business progress with the managers. There were also visits to those members of Mary's family who had remained close to her, but other than these contacts there was little socialising. From the day she opened the new Wentworth in 1928, Mary had made it her world and her busy schedule left little time for outside interests. I'm sure that if it had been suggested she did not go out enough, she would have hastened to say that she had all the people and all the conversation she wanted right under her own roof. What is more, Mary worked long hours, and preferred to save her energy for what she considered important. This explains why she did not have the circle of friends most women gather around them over a lifetime. When Mary died, only one published tribute was placed by other than family, staff and lessees.

Mary was never a member of the Hotel Association, or United Licensed Victuallers' Association, as it was then called - surprising, considering her large stake in the industry. However, this fact is further evidence of the independent spirit which would not allow her to be regimented by what others thought. She solved her own problems.

Mary was often approached by agents with city properties for sale. She was continually on the lookout for suitable investments and Joe enjoyed the new experience of inspecting these with his wife.

Mary never intended that Joe would be her partner in name only - either in respect to managing the Wentworth and her other properties, or in sharing ownership with her. She was anxious to demonstrate this to him as well as to those relations who continued to look upon Joe as an outsider.

A section of Mary's family was very much against the marriage, hastily deciding that Joe was an opportunist who had married Mary for her money. The fact that he was thirteen years her junior probably fuelled this speculation. There was even a claim that Mary did not know what she was doing and was no longer capable of managing her own affairs or those of Metropolitan Properties and United Service Hotel Co Ltd. Such a suggestion was ludicrous, but at a time when she expected her family to share her happiness in finding the right partner, it caused her a great deal of anguish.

Early in 1944, Mary decided to give Joe shares in United Service Hotel Co Ltd. In order to pre-empt possible opposition Mary asked two of her sisters, Laura (Lolly) Cooke and Elsie Norchi, each of whom held 2,000 shares, to return them to her at a nominal cost. The shares had been a gift from their sister and they agreed without hesitation.[5] Her brother George pledged to support any decision she made in respect of the companies, whilst preferring to retain his shareholding. Mary thought she had won the day and arranged the legal formalities to transfer 4,000 shares to Joe's name.

The early victory was not the end of the matter, but there was a period of calm before the storm.

Early in 1944, within a few months of Mary's marriage to Joe, there were increasingly hopeful signs that the war which had dominated the collective thought and energy for almost five years, was nearing its end. However, the then Prime Minister, John Curtin, warned against complacency and said that there were still some tough times ahead. Despite the Prime Minister's warning, throughout 1944 newspaper reports were increasingly optimistic. If one thing bolstered the confidence of a people longing for a return to peace it was the gradual release of army personnel back into civilian life. By the end of April 1944 almost 14,450 servicemen had been returned to primary and other essential industries and the releases were seen to be ongoing.

In Perth there was certainly evidence of a reduced US Navy presence. It was impossible for Mary to be unaware of the lessening call on accommodation. Her queries as to the reason were explained away by claims that on completing patrols submarines were returning directly to home ports for service and maintenance, rather than stopping off at Fremantle.

At the same time, as less and less accommodation was required at the Wentworth, it soon became evident that something more significant was happening.

The US submariners had come to Perth without fuss or fanfare, two and a half years later they left just as silently. The first official notification of their withdrawal appeared in *The West Australian* on 23 October 1944. It was a copy of a report published in the *New York Times* two days earlier, written by Frank Kluckhohn, a war correspondent attached to General MacArthur's staff.

> It may now be revealed that the American Army and Navy have evacuated Australia completely, except for a few skeleton supply units, after a friendly invasion lasting 2½ years.
> When the first main body of Americans reached Australia they were received with wide acclaim and all doors were opened to them. As the American contingent grew, civilian difficulties increased and some inevitable points of friction developed. Australians as a whole demonstrated restraint and hospitality, although enthusiasm naturally waned in crowded troops areas.
> It is probably fair to state that as the Americans leave, Australia is more unreservedly pro-Empire than ever before. Many personal friendships have been forged that will stand the test of time, many Americans will always have a soft spot in their hearts for Australia, while the many marriages between Australian girls and Americans have created a permanent link.
> It is anyone's guess what long range effect the friendly invasion will have on relations between Australia and America. It is my guess that in the long run the pleasant joint experiences will be remembered and inevitable unpleasantnesses that must occur under such circumstances will be forgotten.

This was probably an excellent summation of a situation that has claimed the attention of writers for past decades. However, it is social commentary. During the course of the war, a total of eleven American submarines were lost on patrols out of Fremantle and it is impossible to know what part the US presence had played in shielding Australia from being more directly involved in the horrors of the conflict.

The official notification that our American allies were departing, brought an upsurge of speculation that the declaration of peace was

Courtesy The Raine Foundation

Mary Raine circa 1935

imminent. At the least, it signalled that the Japanese advance had been contained.

Just two weeks before the American authorities surrendered their claims at the Wentworth, and accommodation and dining room facilities returned to their normal status, Mary and Joe received a surprise visit from the Chairman of the State Licensing Court. He advised that complaints had been received from members of the public that over a long period it had not been possible to secure accommodation at two of their hotels, namely, the Wentworth in Perth and the Windsor in South Perth. He went on to remind them that if licensed premises were occupied by our own or Allied Services, and therefore unable to comply with accommodation requirements governing the licence to sell liquor, then such licence would be withdrawn until the requirements were met.

What the Chairman said carried a veiled ultimatum and Mary was not particularly happy about it. After all, she had not wanted to surrender the residential side of the hotel, but had been persuaded that it was her duty to do so and now she was being threatened with the closure of the most important part of their business. Fortunately, before she had put her mind to countering the attack, the US Navy administration terminated the agreement with the Wentworth. Once the threat had passed, it was easy for Mary and Joe to appreciate the humour of the situation. They found it almost inconceivable, that for two and a half years the Licensing Court had been unaware that residential facilities in most of Perth's larger hotels had been requisitioned by the visiting Allies.[6]

In some ways Mary was disappointed she did not need to lock horns with the local bureaucracy on this issue. It represented the kind of battle she relished - fighting stupidity with common sense and logic. There could be nothing more ridiculous than removing a hotel licence in wartime because accommodation was provided for our own or allied servicemen!

On 8 May 1945 came the longed-for announcement. The headlines of *The West Australian* proclaimed the joyous news that hostilities in Europe had ended with the final defeat of Germany and unconditional surrender of her forces on all fronts.

Perth erupted as excited crowds took to the streets. Strangers hugged and kissed in the elation of the moment and spontaneous celebrations broke out all over the city.

However, the war with Japan continued, and Australians were possibly more mindful of this than their joyous Allies in the United Kingdom. During the preceding months, much had been published about how long it might take to defeat Japan after Germany surrendered and all forecasts warned that this would not be accomplished swiftly. Estimating from the wealth of information available to it, the Office of War Information (OWI) stated publicly that crushing Japan would require a minimum of eighteen to twenty-four months after Germany's defeat.

Thankfully, these gloomy predictions were not realised. It was just three more painful months before the dream of total peace became a reality. On 6 August 1945 an American B29 aircraft took off from the Western Pacific island of Tinian carrying a new and devastating weapon of war - an atomic bomb. It had the force of 20,000 tons of normal high explosive. The dropping of this bomb on the Japanese city of Hiroshima, followed within days by the similar bombing of Nagasaki, finally achieved an end to the conflict. No war in history ever ended with such a catastrophic and shattering climax. Did the end justify the means? History will judge. Suffice to say, the event was so traumatic that reports of the first bomb dropped were more sombre than euphoric.

> The West Australian 8 August 1945
>
> Washington 7 August
>
> The atomic bomb dropped by an American airman on Hiroshima yesterday has echoed around the world. Its effect on future world strategy is already being discussed in high military circles, where the need for rigid control of its manufacture and use is conceded. Its present use against Japan as an aggressor nation is justified, the general belief being that it will shorten the war and save thousands of Allied lives. Some, however, see in the new weapon of destruction a sinister shadow over the future of humanity.

Japan's response came quickly with an offer of surrender on 11 August. For those who missed the news on their radios, the pealing of the bells from St George's Cathedral rang out the message the world had been longing to hear. The announcement was met with a strange mixture of gaiety and solemnity, resulting as it did from the use of a weapon of such cruel devastation that most people were yet to come to terms with whether it was right or wrong to use it.

On Wednesday 15 August 1945 came the official declaration that victory had been achieved in the Pacific theatre of war. A parade held the following day attracted a hundred thousand people to the centre of Perth. The crowd included Americans in uniform mingling with the 7,000 marching servicemen and women.

Two months before the cessation of hostilities, Mary became aware that she had her own private war to contend with. As she suspected, the matter of the United Service Hotel shares transferred to Joe in 1944 had not really been resolved.

The Chairman of United Service Hotel Co Ltd, Mary's nephew, Frederick Ernest Carter, one of the shareholders who objected to Joe's ownership of shares, called a meeting for 12 June 1945. He had put in place a plan to increase the number of directors from three to four and to remove Mary from her position as secretary of the company. The 'numbers' showed both motions would be successful.

Mary and Joe were warned of this development and absented themselves from the meeting. Mr John Philip Durack (Solicitor) attended as proxy for Joe. Also absent was Mr Arthur Valentine Rutherford (Val) Abbott (Solicitor) who was represented by Mr Claude Robert McWilliam (Bank Manager).

The issue of increasing the number of directors was introduced by the chairman, and it was moved by Mr Sidney Frederick Carter (Mary's brother), seconded by Mrs Millicent Ainsworth (Mary's niece), that the number of directors be increased from three to four.

After recorded objections from Mr Durack and Mr McWilliam the motion was carried.

Mrs Ainsworth then nominated Mrs Irene Elsie Marsh (Mary's niece, sister of Mrs Ainsworth and F E Carter) to be appointed a director of the company. Mr S F Carter seconded the resolution, and it was duly carried.

Half of the 'secret agenda' had already been achieved. The meeting continued, with a transparent move by the chairman to nullify the allocation of shares to Joe.

The following is quoted from a copy of the minutes of the meeting. Errors are unedited. The minutes speak for themselves and I have refrained from making editorial comment.

> **The Chairman:**
> The next matter on the agenda is to remove the present secretary and appoint a new secretary of the Company.
> As Chairman of Directors I would like to point out there has not been a General Meeting held, I think, for nearly two years. A copy of the Minutes shows that the last meeting of Directors was really not held - the Minutes are unsigned in the Minute Book. The matter is serious from the standpoint of law in regard to the Company. It also leaves this Company open to its actions being considered as not being quite on behalf of the shareholders. As a matter of fact, I regard it very seriously. The Secretary should at least have advised the Directors in regard to that meeting. I myself received no notice of the meeting, though my name appears there, and I was not even present.
> The business transacted at that meeting - if it was - was quite illegal, in my opinion. I don't know if you agree with me in regard to Company Law, but it leaves us very very open. I think the Secretary either is not interested, or probably does not appreciate the position in regard to this Company. That is why this motion is before this Meeting now. I will throw it open for discussion and call for a resolution in regard to it, to remove the present Secretary and appoint a new Secretary.
> **Mr McWilliam:**
> Mrs Raine is the Secretary. She has been father and mother to this Company. She bought the property. She gave you people your shares.
> **The Chairman:**
> I object to that. I have worked very hard for mine.
> **Mr. McWilliam:**
> Nevertheless she started this Company. She has been father and

mother to the Company. She has been secretary for many years.

Mr Brian George Carter (Mary's brother):

I think, morally the United Service belongs to Mrs Raine; legally it might belong to the shareholders. I have worked for her for many years and have always been paid for my services. I think it is outrageous to remove Mrs Raine. I think I can say I am one of the few members of the family who keep in contact with her. She was very, very upset. Apparently the fly in the ointment appears to be that she got married again. Had she remained single F.E.Carter would have been as thick as ever.

Mr S.F.Carter:

I think this is rather irrelevant to the meeting. I suggest that Mr George Carter is here today because on 30 June there is a licence of an hotel going to be transferred to him which at the present time Mrs Thomas holds. That might be the reason he is speaking that way.

Mr McWilliam:

I can answer that. It is the practice to renew all licences at 30 June. Mr Carter already holds that licence. It is common practice to renew a licence on 30th June.

Mr Durack:

These matters are entirely irrelevant. I think Mrs Raine's service to the Company is relevant, and what she has done for the Company is what we should discuss now - not what any individual shareholder should expect to get.

The Chairman:

I have pointed out that the last meeting of Directors, when I was not present, is in the Minute book.

Mr Durack:

What is there in the meeting supposed to have taken place that is objected to?

The Chairman:

I will read you the minutes. They are undated.

Although I was not present at that meeting, that transfer was afterwards approved by me, or I signed the share scrip certificate presented to me. I did not know my name appeared as at the meeting. I thought Mr S.F. Carter was present - it said one Mr Carter. So I signed on behalf of the Company, understanding that the meeting was held and approved.

Mr Durack:

Do you bring that up against Mrs Raine?

The Chairman:

You admitted yourself that it is not the practice in Company Law to have minutes undated in the Minute Book.'

Mr Durack:
She does not sign Minutes.
The Chairman:
Is it within the law to say a Director is present when he is not?
Mr Durack:
These Minutes were probably typed after you signed the transfer, in which event it could quite honestly be put that you were present. Now you are suggesting that Mrs Raine did something illegal.
The Chairman:
I would like you to note the date of it and the date the scrip was signed.
Mr Durack:
It must have been subsequent to that going through. Mrs Raine has not done anything illegal by assuming you were present.
The Chairman:
I am saying the affairs of the Company have been loosely run.
Mr Durack:
Why? Because she did not put the date of the meeting? I think it is a wrong accusation.
Mr S.F.Carter:
It is for the shareholders to say whether they are satisfied or whether they are not.
Mr Durack:
Representing a shareholder, I am entitled to know why, and the reasons why it is alleged she is unsatisfactory as a secretary.
The Chairman:
I have tried to give you the reasons.
Mr S.F. Carter:
I move:- That the conduct of the present secretary, Mrs Mary Bertha Raine, is not satisfactory to the majority of the shareholders of the Company, and that the Directors therefore wish to remove her from office and appoint a new secretary.
Mrs Ainsworth:
I second that.
Mr McWilliam:
You are rushing into something rather fast. I suggest that you give a little thought to this action before you take such a drastic step.
The Chairman:
The resolution is moved and seconded.
Mr McWilliam:
It is very easy to come to a hasty decision of that kind, but you have certain things at stake. Why do something you might regret

later? The present secretary has carried out her duties. She might not be the best in the world, but she has done a good job in the interests of the Company.

The Chairman:

There is a motion before the Meeting that this Company remove the Secretary.

Mr Durack:

You may now dismiss Mrs Raine as secretary of this Company and appoint another one. Has this meeting stopped to think what Mrs Raine might be able to do to the Company tomorrow morning? And has this Meeting been properly informed as to the position Mrs Raine holds in regard to the Company and the Company to her? As a shareholder I am entitled to ask what that position is, and what might be the effect of that action? It might be quite easy to dismiss Mrs Raine now as secretary and at the same time it might be that Mrs Raine can dismiss the whole Company tomorrow. Why should not the members of the Company be properly informed as to the situation?

I understand that Mrs Raine has advanced to the Company very large sums of money. If she has not actually advanced them herself, she has given authority, and they have been advanced at her request, and there are documents signed by the Company to Mrs Raine. If you are going to throw the Company straight into litigation by passing this resolution, I think you would be well advised to stop and think.

The Chairman:

You have all heard Mr Durack.

I will put the motion:-

That this Meeting expresses dissatisfaction with the conduct of the present secretary, Mrs Mary Bertha Raine, and remove her from office and appoint a new secretary.

Motion put to Meeting and carried by a show of hands.

The Chairman:

I think the Meeting is now closed.

There will be a Directors' Meeting immediately afterwards, which Mrs Marsh will attend.

When Mary heard the outcome of the meeting she was furious. Yes, she had taken short cuts when handling the affairs of United Service Hotel Co Ltd. Yes, she had personally arranged an infusion of funds when they were needed. Yes, she had by-passed meetings and prepared back-dated minutes. However, every shareholder was aware of these technical 'misdemeanours' and there had never been a dissenting voice - never, that is, until she married Joe. Was this sorry saga nothing more than an elaborate ploy to wrest control of the Company from her and to nullify Joe's shareholding?

Mary was not only angry, she felt betrayed, and bitterly disappointed that members of her family for whom she had done so much would turn on her in this way. They soon learned they had taken on a formidable adversary. She took immediate steps to regain control.

On 14 September 1945, Abbott and Abbott, of 42 St George's Terrace, Perth, solicitors for Mary and Joe, issued the following writ in the Supreme Court of Western Australia.

> Between
>
> Arnold Yeldham Raine — Plaintiff
>
> and
>
> Irene Elsie Rosalind Marsh
> Sydney Frederick Carter
> United Service Hotel Ltd — Defendants
>
> To Irene Elsie Rosalind Marsh of 2 Francis Street Mount Lawley in the State of Western Australia Married Woman and Sydney Frederick Carter of 18 King Edward Street Osborne Park Poultry Farmer and United Service Hotel Limited whose registered Office is situated at the Office of Messrs Stone James and Co of Furnival Chambers St George's Terrace Perth.
>
> We command you that within ten days after the service of this Writ on you inclusive of the day of such service you do cause an appearance to be entered for you in an action at the suit of Arnold Yeldham Raine and take notice that in default of your doing so the Plaintiff may proceed therein and judgment may be given in your absence.
>
> Witness. The Honourable Sir John Alfred Northmore KCMG Chief Justice of Western Australia this 14th day of September 1945
>
> Claim
>
> The Plaintiff's claim is as a shareholder of the United Service Hotel Limited for -

1. A declaration that the Defendants Irene Elsie Rosalind March and Sydney Frederick Carter were not legally and properly elected directors of the United Service Hotel Limited and are not directors of the said Company.
2. A declaration that any resolution carried at any meeting of directors of the said Company at which the said Irene Elsie Marsh or the said Sydney Frederick Carter were present and where the presence of both or either of them was necessary to form a quorum or at which they took part in the deliberations is void and of no effect.
3. An injunction restraining the said Irene Elsie Marsh and the said Sydney Frederick Carter from acting as directors of the said Company,
4. FURTHER or other relief.
5. Costs

The Notice of Appearance was issued for 21 September 1945

The summons had been taken out in the heat of the moment, and on reflection Mary realised the battle could be won by taking a more direct approach. Litigation was anathema to Mary - a course she preferred to avoid at all costs, the waste of money appalled her. She discussed her options with Solicitor John Durack, who had represented Joe at the fateful meeting and was conversant with all the facts. It was decided he should go to the eastern States and confer with lawyer John Fullagar, an expert on company law. The lawyer, who later became well known as Mr Justice Fullagar of the High Court of Australia, established that the proceedings of the meeting and the directors' meeting which followed, were invalid.

The following year, 1945, George and Jack sold their shares back to Mary. Those members of her family who had worked together to claim control of the United Service Co remained as shareholders. Most held parcels of 3,000 shares. When the University of Western Australia became the majority shareholder on Mary's death in 1960, the shares were bought back. The price paid per share was in the order of eight dollars and the descendants of those who surrendered their shares at Mary's request, refer wryly to the fortunate 'other side of the family' as the 'twenty-four-thousanders'![7]

On 19 June 1947, the partnership of Arnold Yeldham and Mary Bertha Raine sold four shops they had acquired personally, to Metropolitan Properties. The total value was £20,500. In lieu of a cash payment the purchaser issued and allotted to each of the vendors 10,250 fully paid £1.0.0 shares in the company. This increased the number of issued shares to 100,000, of which Mary held 56,950 and Joe 29,435.

Mary could never again be subjected to threats from within her company. At the time of her death, the estrangement from most of the family members whom she believed had betrayed her, remained unresolved.

There was a notable exception. Her niece, Millicent Ainsworth who, as a small child, had spent time with Mary and her first husband on the farm at Harvey, always had a special place in Mary's heart. The bonds forged during those early days were strong enough to survive the trauma caused by Millicent's defection, and she was subsequently forgiven and welcomed back into life at the Wentworth. Mary's affection for Millicent and her children continued until her death.

One of Millicent's daughters, Ailsa Raymond of Kingsley, has happy memories of times spent at the hotel in the company of Great-aunt Mary and Joe. The third generation Carter children inherited the family's musical talent and Ailsa recalls that Joe liked nothing better than to get them together with Mary for a sing-song around the piano on Sunday afternoons.[8]

Ailsa also tells about a side of Mary seldom seen by outsiders. She remembers her great-aunt as being naturally warm and affectionate, responding to the boisterous cuddles and kisses of her young great-nieces with equal enthusiasm.[9]

Through Ailsa I also learned that Mary's niece, Irene Marsh, who had lent her support to those opposing Mary at the historic meeting on 12 June 1945, deeply regretted her decision, and expressed remorse on many occasions later in her life.[10]

Following the declaration of peace, Western Australia gradually reverted to pre-war conditions. Men demobilised from the services were quickly absorbed into a labour market hungry for workers and most women left their wartime jobs to resume their accepted role of homemaker.

The withdrawal of the US Navy in October 1944, meant that Mary and Joe had returned the Wentworth to pre-war routine well before the conflict was officially over. It quickly became evident that getting and keeping staff would be an ongoing problem for all businesses trying to return to normal. The Federal Government had foreseen the problem and initiated an immigration policy which, it was hoped, would provide essential labour for the developmental boom anticipated with the cessation of hostilities. The policy was also designed to showcase Australia's readiness to play its part in resettling those left homeless by the war.

The Government's plan targeted displaced persons from the refugee camps of Europe. They were offered assisted passage in return for their agreement to accept a two-year period of directed employment. The first of these immigrants started arriving in 1947, followed in the early 1950s by others from Germany, Italy, Holland, Poland, Greece, Yugoslavia and the United Kingdom. In all, more than nineteen thousand displaced persons settled in Western Australia.

Not surprisingly, all sorts of derogatory names for the newcomers became commonplace, but the Government encouraged the use of 'New Australians' as a collective term and it became widely accepted.

In the past, Mary had never found it difficult to retain staff, even though she was a demanding employer and not easily pleased. Occasionally, new employees didn't survive the period of probation, but once a new recruit realised that 'Mrs Raine's bark was worse than her bite', staff settled in and many became long-term employees.

Nell Bowles of Bibra Lake, who worked at the Wentworth during the war years, remembers both Mary and Joe as fair and approachable employers. 'You could talk to either of them if you had a problem.'[11]

Ivy Hogan of Leederville was a very junior waitress at the Gordons Hotel in 1927 and stayed on when it became the remodeled Wentworth Hotel. She remembers those times well.

> Mary Raine, or Ma Thomas as she was at that time, was a very fair employer, but she was also a strict one, and expected her staff to work hard. However, if things were exceptionally busy she would get into it herself and help get through what had to be done. She never asked anyone to do something she would not do herself .
>
> I can see her now. She was incredibly thin and usually wore a white dress of one style or another, complemented by half a dozen long strings of coloured beads. When she leaned over the tables in the kitchen she would gather the beads in her hand and toss them over her shoulder.
>
> I remember an occasion when she came into the kitchen and found that the cook was drunk. The roast meat was burnt to a crisp and a cherry pie had become an overcooked disaster. Ma Thomas was furious. She pounced on the roast and hurled it to the far side of the room whilst the pie ended up in the cinder catcher under the wood stove. Believe it or not, the cook didn't get the sack!
>
> When their work was finished the kitchen staff were allowed to have a main course, but no desserts. Like all young people, we were perpetually hungry, and would sneak a serve of sweets from time to time. If we saw Ma Thomas coming, the sweets would be thrown into the nearest bucket, and we would be innocent as angels when she spoke to us.
>
> On Sundays she would ask one of the permanent guests to drive her out of town to pick decorations for the dining room tables. Twigs from gum trees were favourites because they usually lasted a week.
>
> When I think back to those days it is not surprising that Ma Thomas became a very wealthy woman. She looked twice at every shilling she spent, and expected what was bought for the kitchen to stretch and stretch and stretch!
>
> Of course, she didn't make her fortune by careful catering alone, but by astute business deals and entrepreneurial ventures that placed her well ahead of her time.
>
> It is interesting to think that I once worked for a lady who has made such a big contribution to the State of Western Australia.[12]

Good yardmen were hard to find, and harder still to keep. When Joe had been left in the lurch by yet another who had seemed promising, he decided to contact the Department of Immigration and see if a New Australian was available for the job. The Department sent Vaclav Novak, who had just arrived from Czechoslovakia. From day one, he became 'Jacko' and was never known by any other name. Joe had the job of teaching the new man the ropes, as well as the English language, and the two developed a close working relationship. Jacko could rely on Joe to protect him from Mary's wrath when his work hadn't measured up to scratch, or when he had a few too many beers before coming on duty. He remained at the Wentworth until the hotel passed into the hands of the University of Western Australia.

Soon after their marriage, Mary and Joe had decided that a new car was not a luxury, but a necessity. Joe's trusty ute was hardly suitable and had become Jacko's runabout, and Mary and Joe had come to rely on taxis for short trips in and about the city. An order was placed with Winterbottom Motors for a new Austin A40 Sheerline, a luxury sedan, on the drawing board for early post-war production. When advice came from the company that the vehicle had arrived, Joe couldn't wait to get behind the wheel. It was a sleek, silver-grey monument to British excellence in prestige automobile manufacture, with the luxurious interior smelling tantalisingly of new leather and polished walnut. Joe's Austin was the first of the new model delivered into Western Australia after the war.[13]

The acquisition of new properties was never far from Mary's mind, and towards the end of the 1940s she and Joe bought Marlborough House, a large private hotel on the corner of Hay and George Streets, west of the main city precinct. Mary felt confident they could upgrade the premises and obtain a full hotel licence for it. Whilst working towards this goal they received an offer representing an excellent profit on the purchase, and accepted it. The premises eventually became the fully licensed George Hotel, subsequently demolished to make way for the Mitchell Freeway.

Barney Richards of Floreat, an accountant doing Mary Raine's work at this time, remembers her well.

I was working for the accounting firm of Paton and Morris when it took over Mary Raine's work in 1946. Prior to that time Mary Raine did her own taxation returns. She had a brilliant brain and was exceptionally quick with figures. The only fault I found in the returns she had prepared was the omission of the £78 required to be shown by hotel keepers for their own board and lodging - an error she had inadvertently repeated for five years. The omission fuelled an investigation by the Taxation Department, and this was probably the reason she decided to let an accountant handle her affairs.

There was a lot of graft in those days, and it flourished in the field of starting price bookmaking, which was illegal. Every hotel, the Wentworth among them, had its own SP bookie operating behind the licensed premises. It was part of life and was tolerated by the police - up to a point. Every so often there would be a raid, but police would give warning beforehand. A paid 'stooge', often a pensioner, would stand in for the regular bookmaker, be arrested and pay the fine. The regular would be back on his pitch as soon as the 'stooge' had been taken away.

There were always stories going the rounds - which may, or may not have been true - about overcoats with large sums of money in the pockets being hung on hotel racks. Police would come in, hang one coat and leave with the other. The Wentworth was said to play this game along with many other hotels.

I was responsible for Mary Raine's work for just two years, but she made a lasting impression on me. In my mind she stands out from the many clients I worked for over the years. She had always calculated her own bar percentages, but after she married Joe she taught him to do the sums. I was probably the only other person she allowed to do this. She would say. 'I trust Barney because he doesn't drink.'[14]

Chapter 8

It's the best room in the hotel

1948 - 1949

Mary and Joe Raine had been married less than five years, when they became part of my life in 1948. My own marriage to Eric (Cole) Sangster had taken place just three months earlier on 21 February 1948, in Newcastle, New South Wales. The wedding date had been changed from April, so we could leave together when Cole accepted a promotion requiring a move to Western Australia. He was working for the Western Electric Company at the time and was to open a new State branch in Perth.

Although it was three years since the end of the war, the post-war housing shortage was a problem facing almost all newly-weds. It was accepted practice for young couples to move in with the parents of one or the other until such time as a home of their own became available. Being aware of this, Cole and I were very anxious about what arrangements the company had made for our accommodation in Perth.

The question was foremost in our thoughts when we met with the General Manager for a pre-departure briefing in Sydney on the day we were due to fly west. He was faintly amused at our concern and confidently assured us that unlike all other States in Australia, Western Australia did not have a housing shortage. He went so far as to say that we would be able to choose from a whole range of options, and for this reason the company had not made any commitments on our behalf. It did sound as if we were off to Utopia. However, as subsequent events proved, the information on the availability of accommodation could not have been further from the truth.

We arrived in Perth on a warm, still evening in May. The Sydney we left behind was in the throes of an accepted post-war inconvenience - power rationing. Consequently, sections of the city had power only on the basis of one hour on, one hour off, resulting in a permanent pall over the metropolis after dark. I had forgotten what a city could look like, bathed in a sea of light. As our plane gradually slowed and lost altitude in preparation for landing, I leaned into the small window, watching eagerly for a first glimpse of the city that was to be our new home. As the twinkling lights increased and multiplied, forming a glowing carpet beneath us, I felt I had never looked down on anything quite so beautiful.

Thus began my love affair with Perth, and through all the ups and downs of the past fifty-odd years, I have never wavered from my conviction that those who spend their lives here are privileged.

Our plane for the flight west was the flagship of Australian National Airways (later known as Ansett Airways), the Skymaster *Amana*. Just two years later on 26 June 1950, it crashed near York soon after take-off from Perth Airport, bound for Adelaide and Sydney, with twenty-four passengers and five crew on board. At the time, it was the worst disaster in Australian Civil Aviation history. The sole survivor from the flaming wreckage, which was reported to have burned for hours, died in hospital soon after.

Opting for the least expensive way to get from the airport to the city, we boarded the airline's courtesy coach. This took us to the main office, located at the time in William Street between Hay Street and St George's Terrace, next to the Palace Hotel. Recalling the occasion now, I find it hard to believe that more than half a century has passed since we were asking the clerk if he would look after our luggage until we found some place to stay. Here we were, on the other side of Australia, knowing no one and with nowhere to go.

The effects of the long trip - it was a long trip back in 1948 - and the tension of facing an uncertain future, were beginning to take their toll. However, we mustered our sense of adventure and set off to find somewhere to put our heads down for the night. We walked along William Street towards Wellington Street, noting briefly, that the Wentworth Hotel looked nice, but expensive. Further along, the Royal Hotel on the Wellington Street corner presented a possibility, but the tariff quoted was way too high. Back to Murray Street, where we turned east and tried our luck at the Australia, long since demolished and passed into pub history. We continued on to the Criterion and Savoy Hotels in Hay Street, but in each case, the prices were well beyond our limited means. At this stage, we had traversed the city square and were back at our starting point opposite the Wentworth Hotel. With nothing to lose, we decided to check out the tariff.

To the right of the entrance, we approached a long, rather forbidding reception desk, attended by a short, stout, unsmiling lady of doubtful vintage. Cole explained that we needed accommodation, not just for the night, but possibly for quite some time.

'Do you offer a special tariff under these circumstances? We will need all meals.'

We were advised brusquely, that the charge for double accommodation, with full board, was £4.5.0 per week, payable in advance. It seemed a very fair tariff for a hotel which looked so inviting from the outside. Almost fearing to jeopardise our good fortune, I ventured a tentative question.

'Is it a nice room?'

'It's the best room in the hotel,' was the curt reply. And indeed, as I discovered later, it was.

The lady introduced herself as 'Mrs Boom', adding that she would show us upstairs after we had collected our luggage. I was yet to learn that no one went upstairs at the Wentworth without suitcases.

In no time at all we were installed in room seven, on the William Street frontage of the first floor, with bathroom and toilet facilities almost opposite. We were pleased to find the room contained a handbasin with both hot and cold water, a luxury not usually found in hotel rooms at the tariff we were paying.

The decision to book into the Wentworth was monumental, for two reasons. First, it moved me into the life of a woman who was certainly the most unforgettable character I have ever met, and secondly, it determined the course of our lives for the next twenty-two years.

With the accommodation problem solved, at least in the short term, the tension and anxiety fell away, replaced by the sense of elation and expectancy that comes with new beginnings. I started to unpack. Cole wondered out loud if it would be possible to get a beer.

'It's very late,' I said, hoping to discourage him.

'Not really. The bars don't close until 9 o'clock over here. Anyway, we are booked in. We should be able to get a drink. I'll ask at the desk, and if it's OK I'll come up and get you.' He was back in minutes.

'The owners are serving house guests in the lounge. It's a good chance to meet them. Come on. Leave the unpacking 'til later.'

Mrs Boom made the introductions; no Christian names in those days. Mr and Mrs Raine, met Mr and Mrs Sangster from New South Wales. We joined a small circle standing around a high desk, dominated by a large cash register. Mary Raine sat on a stool behind it. It was difficult for me to estimate her age, but I now know she was seventy one. She was very tall, somewhat gaunt, bean-thin, and slightly stooped. Her hair, an unusual corn colour, was worn short and slightly waved. Traces of a former fragile beauty remained in her fine facial features and creamy, almost transparent, skin. From her vantage point, Mary led the discussion and responded to her husband's amusing comments with a throaty chuckle.

Joe Raine was obviously younger than his wife. He was a big man, tall, upright and robust. He seemed to be genuinely interested in meeting us, asking all sort of questions about where we came from, and why we were in WA. He was perfect in his role of a jovial, welcoming host.

The session finished at about 11.00 p.m. I had enjoyed myself too much to feel tired whilst caught up in the excitement of the evening, but when we finally retreated to the quiet of our room, I could scarcely struggle through the motions of getting ready for bed. We slept for the next ten hours.

The first weeks were busy. Cole started looking for suitable offices for his company and selected rooms in the heart of St George's Terrace, almost next door to the building where Perpetual Trustees is still located. I was in the happy situation of being left to my own devices to learn about our new home, and I explored it on foot and by tram, with an occasional ferry ride across to South Perth to visit the Zoo. I never missed an opportunity to strike up a conversation and to learn as much as I could about Western Australia and the people who lived here. From hearsay, I had been led to believe that Perth people were the friendliest in Australia and I soon found the description to be correct.

Unlike today, where the city is a cosmopolitan mix of people from all over the world, non-Western Australians were a rarity in 1948. The locals were not much interested in which State you hailed from. You were, quite simply, an 'Eastern Stater'. I was amazed to discover that so few of the people we met had ever been outside Western Australia, losing sight of the fact that no one I could remember back in Newcastle had ever been to Perth!

The degree of attention we received from both management and staff certainly didn't reflect the meagre tariff we were paying. Joe and Mary were very good to us. Joe drove an iridescent silver Austin A40. He told us proudly, it was the first of its kind to be delivered after the war. We had heard a whisper that privileged guests were sometimes invited to enjoy Joe's 'grand tour', and when he suggested we might like to see the sights, we accepted with enthusiasm.

Joe was in his element pointing out Perth's special attractions as we followed that still popular tourist route, along Mounts Bay

Road, around the river at Crawley, through Dalkeith, Peppermint Grove, Mosman Park and on to Fremantle, returning on the southern side and back to the city over the causeway. It was easy for me to love everything about Perth.

Quite soon after our arrival, Mary asked if we were interested in football. 'There's a special match today. We call it a derby, when East Perth plays West Perth, and if you'd like to watch a good game, this is the one to see. The East Perth ground isn't far from the city, but you need to go fairly early to get a seat. I'll pack a lunch for you.'

It was a very gracious offer. How could we refuse? Cole had been to football matches in Victoria and had a small knowledge of the game. He explained to me that it was quite different from the game of rugby, which was the most popular code in New South Wales. Mary sent us off with corned beef and pickle sandwiches, large wedges of fruit cake, oranges and bananas. At the time, I didn't fully appreciate how honoured we were. This gesture was not part of the regular service

During the next few weeks, we met a number of Mary's family members, most of whom had emigrated to Western Australia under her sponsorship. In 1949 she welcomed her niece, Mary Coward, with husband Dick, and family, who arrived to settle in Perth. Mary Coward was the eldest daughter of Mary's sister, Laura (Lolly) Cooke.

Mary Coward remembers the early years.

> My mother, Mary Raine's second youngest sister, was a schoolgirl when big sisters Mary, (or 'Birdie' as she was called), and Daisy went to Australia. Apparently Birdie was a child with a very inquiring mind. My mother remembered her pouring water through the holes in a cane chair to see where it went!
> It seems Birdie did not get on well with her father, but loved her mother very much, and supported her in shouldering responsibility for the younger members of the family. Life could not have been easy for her.
> I had met Birdie only once, whilst still a schoolgirl, before my husband Dick and I came to Australia in 1949. Birdie nominated

us and we stayed with her at the Wentworth for five months, as it was very difficult to find accommodation in Perth in those early post-war years.

Birdie got on very well with Dick. She enjoyed talking to him about the share market, and they had long discussions when he helped her in the hotel at night, as some return for putting us up. We left the Wentworth in January 1950, to live in an old house Birdie owned in Bowman Street, South Perth. It was occupied by pre-war tenants who paid between ten and twelve shillings per week rent. They were protected by law from rent increases or eviction. It was a large house and we became the fifth tenants. Soon after we moved there we started looking for a home of our own and bought one in the same area. We made the mistake of finalising the purchase without consulting Birdie. When she saw it, she was adamant that it would not do, and put it back in the hands of the agent before we plucked up the courage to argue. It was sold for fifty pounds less than we had paid for it, and at the time that represented a huge loss.

Eventually we decided to buy the Bowman Street house. No one knew us and, although Dick was a pharmacist, it was impossible to get a loan from a bank. Birdie came to the rescue and went guarantor for us.

Birdie mixed a generous spirit with a hard head for business, and kept the two sentiments quite separate in her mind. She lent us some money to buy shares. When they went up and we sold them, she kept only the original loan, giving us the profit. On the other hand, if we called at the Wentworth and bought a drink or a meal, we would be charged at the normal rate. Birdie made no allowance for the times she arrived at our home with a retinue of acquaintances, and expected to be given lunch!

The first Christmas we were in Perth, whilst we were still at the Wentworth, we caught a bus to City Beach, not realising the buses stopped at midday. When we rang to say we were stranded, Birdie's only comment was, 'Good. I'll put two extra people at your table.' Fair enough, I guess. We did eventually get a taxi back, in time for a rather belated meal.

At the time the Wentworth had some rather odd visitors, including a lady from the Royal Show who ate with her feet. Birdie feared our three year old daughter might comment and moved us to another table. She needn't have worried. The lady was so skilful, no one would have noticed.

Birdie suffered frequently from illness, but never let it affect her judgment. She drove herself hard and disliked giving in to weakness. As relatives we probably did not realise at the time what a unique personality she had become.[1]

Rather like examining a precious stone. When you get too close you fail to detect the sparkle.

We had an open invitation to join the regular close-of-day gathering with Joe and Mary, and rarely failed to do so. Western Australia along with Queensland, was a forerunner in liberalising hotel drinking hours. Coming from the infamous 'six o'clock swill' of the eastern States, we expected to see signs of more civilised drinking behaviour where nine o'clock closing had been introduced two years earlier. However, in all honesty, I have to admit that only the hour had changed. Closing time each evening approached bedlam in the Wentworth lounge. Stewardesses battled their way through crowded tables, delivering double rounds before Joe called the dreaded, 'time, gentlemen, please', signalling that the day's drinking was over.

It is strange that the busier a place of entertainment is, the more people will battle to get inside. The Wentworth lounge was always packed. The fact that live entertainment was on offer both in the afternoons and evenings, may have had a lot to do with its popularity. When visiting US naval vessels were berthed in Fremantle, the personnel made a bee-line for the hotel, and claimed it as their own until the day of departure. Mary welcomed the extra business, but the sailors could become unruly and the lounge required constant supervision when they were in town.

The lounge trade generated big money. Small wonder Mary made it her special domain. When all available chairs were occupied, she would carry extra seating from the foyer and dining- room herself, hoisting the heavy chairs above her head and over seated customers, in search of a vacant space. Mary may have looked frail, but she would weave between the tables, carrying her burden with the agility of a person half her age.

When the last rounds of drinks were served, the stewardesses downed trays, and picked up brooms. The flurry of activity encouraged stragglers to get moving.

With the lounge cleared, Mary relaxed visibly and settled down to enjoy what was for her, the best part of the day, sipping warm ale (she never called it beer) with Joe and house guests who were lucky enough to be included. She drank little, and today would hardly be described as a 'social' drinker. The glass of beer remained untouched until it reached room temperature, and was then sipped quietly for the next hour. Joe, on the other hand, approached his drinking with relish and gusto. He usually drank beer, but on occasions when he allowed himself an extra indulgence, his choice was Scotch whisky with a beer chaser. This heady mixture was known in the trade as a 'dogbolter'.

Because dinner hour was the time when the bars were at their busiest, Joe seldom went to the dining-room for the evening meal. Tommy, the Filipino chef, had instructions to leave the boss's order on top of the stove when the kitchens were closed for the day. I now realise that the typical meal, often eaten as late as 10.00 p.m., was a dietary disaster. It could be an enormous serve of steak and kidney pudding, Irish stew, braised steak, or roast meat. By today's standards, Joe was dangerously overweight, even for a man designed by nature to be of generous proportions. In the following years he continued to add to his jovial bulk.

During these after-hour sessions Mary seemed to do most of the talking. We were amazed at her detailed recall of past happenings, and the best stories of all were about the series of events that brought her to Perth in the first place. She obviously enjoyed remembering that part of her life and Joe encouraged her to tell us about it. I noticed he seldom spoke of his own early days.

Occasionally, Mary and Joe would include us in discussions about property they had looked at, or were planning to purchase. Early in 1949, Mary was excited about an investment which represented something of a departure from her usual interests. She revealed that they had signed up to buy Bon Marche Arcade, which fronted Barrack Street between Murray and Wellington Streets. I gathered that its special appeal lay in the fact that all the shops, upstairs and at street level, were leased to long-term reliable tenants. Mary was obviously pleased about the acquisition and suggested we go with them the following day to have a look at it. She also mentioned that they had taken a lease of the Governor Broome Hotel, in the same street as the Wentworth, but on the other side of the railway line.

Our hosts at the Wentworth were 'hands on' hotel keepers or should I say, publicans, the job description used at the time. No aspect of the day-to-day running of the hotel escaped Mary's attention, and the smallest expenditure had to be approved by her. She was an early riser, her working day starting in the huge kitchen. Here, crouched in front of one of the roaring wood stoves, and armed with a long pronged fork, she would make toast for the usual quota of some 120 breakfast guests. I have known her do this when the temperature soared around 100 degrees on the old scale, or when she was still ill from the bouts of pneumonia that confined her to bed at regular intervals. A huge electric toaster stood unused. She did not believe in paying for electricity when she could do the job herself at no cost.

When the last guest was served, Mary enjoyed a leisurely breakfast with 'Rainee'. This was followed by a close scrutiny of the hotel booking register, in consultation with Mrs Boom. How many guests were leaving? How many were due to book in? Armed with this information, she headed for the kitchen, where Tommy was waiting, with the contents of the refrigerators lined up on the enormous scrubbed oak tables. Mary viewed the offerings and decided on the day's menus, making up orders for the butcher, grocer and green grocer as she talked.

The Wentworth had its share of staff problems. Sickness, failure to turn up, sudden decisions to leave, to name just a few. Keeping all positions manned was the most difficult part of hotel business. On one occasion when Joe found himself without sufficient staff to open the lounge bar for the evening shift, Cole offered his services. He had a little 'social' experience, and quickly mastered the art of 'pulling' (never to be confused with 'pouring') beer, and mixing drinks. When he was telling me about it at the end of the day, Cole was excited about the experience, and confided for the first time, that it had always been his ambition to run a hotel. I was quite surprised.

It became accepted that Cole could be called on to help out in the bars during a staffing emergency, or to give Mary a break from her self-imposed duty on the lounge desk. At these times I remained in our room, reading.

Cole was very eager to impress Joe and Mary. If he found they needed him, any arrangements we had were cancelled without question. Of course, this had to be at times when he was not required at his office.

One evening, with a full house booked in for dinner, Mary faced a serious shortage of dining-room staff. Cole volunteered *my* services. Nothing in my past had prepared me for the Wentworth kitchen at full throttle, or for scurrying back and forth with plates of soup, entrees, roast dinners, vegetable platters and desserts, then tackling a mountain of dishes such as I had never visualised in my worst nightmares. Somehow I struggled through it. I never heard what Mary thought of my inexperienced efforts. Maybe she decided that if I was not particularly able, at least I was willing.

I found it odd that staff going off duty were required to leave by the front door, passing the main desk as they did so. I learned later that this was to discourage workers from leaving with property that was not their own. I couldn't help noticing that a little woman who worked in the kitchen arrived each morning with a large, flat and obviously empty, shopping bag. She departed in the evening with the same bag bulging so heavily she could hardly support its weight off the floor. How did she escape detention? She didn't. Mary knew there were many mouths to feed at home and chose to turn a blind eye to the obvious pilfering. Mary could be alarmingly severe, but at other times was the proverbial 'soft touch'.

About three months after our arrival at the Wentworth, we had to face the fact that our finances were not in good shape. Because there was established local competition, sales at the Western Electric Company proved slow to gather momentum. As Cole's remuneration was based on retainer plus commission, we had to accept it could be some time before there was much reward for effort. Although the extra money he was earning at the hotel was helpful, it was not enough, and what money I had when I left home was disappearing fast. I decided I had better get a job. A totally unremarkable thing to do today, but in the world I had left behind, girls did not work after marriage.

Virtually every business house in Perth was looking for staff, so I decided to offer my services at the most convenient location. I crossed the road from the Wentworth to what was then Bairds Family Department Store, later to become WA's first Myer Store, and more recently the Hong Kong Trading Centre. Bairds was a labyrinth of counters and display tables. The store stocked everything and lived up to its slogan. 'You can get it at Bairds.' Perhaps they should have added: 'If you can find it'!

I decided to ask about clerical work and was directed to an office that could hardly have changed since the turn of the century. The dinginess and clutter defied description. It was a lacklustre interview, conducted by an expressionless lady who scarcely managed to muster a semblance of interest in me. After I had listed my qualifications for clerical work, she simply looked up and said: 'We need typists.' I repeated that I was looking for clerical work. Her reply: 'We need typists.'

My reply: 'Thank you, I can type.' I learned to type at Bairds and, more importantly, I got paid for it.

What a job! In the bowels of what had to be the most depressing office in the world, a line of six typists sat behind huge, antiquated machines. In the basket to the left of each was deposited the endless collection of mail-order letters, mountains of them arriving all day, every day. The typist's duty was to decipher the orders and type clear concise lists detailing exactly what the customers were asking for. Some letters were incredibly funny, some strangely pathetic.

'Runners' collected the typed lists and collated requirements from throughout the store, ready for dispatch. The mail-order department was huge, the lifeblood of the business.

I stayed at Bairds for about six months, which wasn't a bad effort, given that I was planning my escape from the moment I first took up a position behind my instrument of torture.

The next job application took me to the offices of Flower, Davies and Johnson, located at the western end of Murray Street, still handy to the Wentworth. The advertisement called for a holiday relief worker. The firm was an agent for farm machinery, tractors and engineering parts. Explaining that I was qualified for clerical work and typing, the reply was: 'We need a book keeper.'

My reply: 'Thank you. I can do book keeping.' I learned quickly, and must have learned well. When the girl I was relieving returned, the boss asked me to stay on, and transferred her to other duties.

My talent for getting jobs for which I had no qualifications whatsoever was ultimately to be challenged again, but that was several months down the track.

Along with the hands-on running of the Wentworth, Mary and Joe kept a vigilant eye on the day-to-day running of hotels they had under management The Windsor Hotel in South Perth was in this category. It was one of the few hotels we had visited ourselves. Cole was quite well known as a cricketer, having enjoyed a brief inclusion in the South Australian Sheffield Shield team, and when it was known he was living in Perth, the South Perth Cricket Club approached him with an offer to play for them. The Windsor Hotel was the club's preferred watering hole. At the time, we had no way of knowing the Raines were not satisfied with the performance of the current management team they employed at the hotel.

We had lived at the Wentworth for almost a year and I was still working at Flower, Davies and Johnson, when Cole surprised me with the suggestion that we should try to find less expensive accommodation. He was right, of course. We couldn't go on living as permanent hotel guests. Even though our combined earnings kept us reasonably solvent, there was no way of saving and it was time to think about our future.

Unless money was no object, there were no houses or flats to buy or rent in Perth. Young couples lived with parents or rented a room with use of facilities. The latter was our only option. We consulted the To Let section of the weekend paper and started a dispiriting search for somewhere suitable to live. I shudder at the memory of some of the places we looked at! One, I recall vividly, because Cole was tired of 'looking', and insisted that we accept the bed on the verandah of a house in Cottesloe. The rental was £1.0.0 per week, with use of the bathroom and kitchen. I said 'No,' and refused to budge. 'Surely,' I said between sobs, 'you couldn't ask me to accept this dreadful makeshift as our first home!'

Our future may well have been very different, had I not behaved with uncharacteristic stubbornness.

We settled down to stay on at the Wentworth. Cole went off to his office each day and helped in the bar or lounge most evenings. I continued with my job. However, although the matter was not discussed, the need to move on hung over our heads like a dark cloud.

Our worries must have been apparent to others. Years later, when we enjoyed a close friendship with Paddy Baker, he told us that Mary and Joe had commented to him that the young guests didn't seem as happy as previously.

Chapter 9

We hope you'll say 'Yes'

1949 - 1951

It was Friday afternoon. With the working week behind us, Cole and I were looking forward to the freedom of the next two days. We claimed our favourite chairs in the lounge and had settled in to read the afternoon paper when Joe came and sat with us. 'Have you got a minute? The wife would like a word with you. She's in the office.' It happened too quickly for me to start wondering what the formality was all about. Mary lost no time in saying what was on her mind.

'How would you like to manage the Windsor for us? We intend to make changes over there and Joe and I have discussed the idea that you young people would be ideal for the job. We hope you'll say "Yes".'

I was speechless. Cole could hardly contain his elation. The offer came as a bolt from the blue. This possibility had never even entered our minds. My first concern was that I had no experience, no training. Would I be able to do it? Cole had no such reservations and was accepting the suggestion with enthusiasm. I kept my doubts to myself, not wanting to spoil the excitement of the moment. Mary and Joe were obviously very pleased when it became clear that we were accepting their offer.

Mary continued, 'We want you to take over at the end of the month, the end of the financial year - that's just two weeks from now. Joe will arrange for your Publican's General Licence application to be submitted on Monday, Cole, and get a provisional licence pending the sitting of the Court and the formal approval. We really want the present managers to vacate the premises without delay. Can you both be ready to start as soon as that?'

Cole assured them we could.

'Right then. That's settled. We will help you in any way we can, but you won't have any problems. We know you'll do a good job. Just one thing. It would be quite impossible to run a hotel if you had any family.'

The final comment was almost a throw-away line, but the inference was not lost on me.

When I think back, I realise it was a pretty loose-knit sort of business arrangement, but was probably testimony to the degree of mutual regard between the four of us. Salary, terms and conditions were not even mentioned. These matters were just addressed as the need arose. It would never do in today's world of contracts and workplace agreements.

The following two weeks were feverishly busy. Cole and I had to give notice to our respective employers - much easier for me than for Cole, who had to find a new manager on behalf of his company. It had become obvious he was not enjoying his position with Western Electric, and the prospect of leaving and working in a field that had always held an attraction, gave him new zest. Suddenly all our problems were solved. Board, lodging, all the costs of running a home were now taken care of. An unspoken prayer had been answered. On 30 June 1949, we packed our bags and vacated room seven at the Wentworth, to take up an exciting challenge and begin a new life south of the river.

We were not aware that Cole was the youngest hotel licensee in Western Australia. Back then, the publican's life tended to attract more mature men and women. We were fortunate Mary and Joe did not consider age had anything to do with potential ability.

We were not prepared for the reception that awaited us on our arrival at the Windsor. The outgoing managers were understandably unhappy about their summary dismissal. Mary and Joe had not discussed their reasons with us, and it would be unfair to dwell on possible scenarios. However, although we were in no way responsible, the departing management team probably felt they had to vent their anger on someone. Their way of getting even was to make everything as difficult as possible. I walked into an office with not a scrap of paper in sight. Every record of the day-to-day running of the hotel had been removed or destroyed. No guests' register, day book, rosters, paybooks, ledgers, stock books - nothing. We were too happy to be daunted. When you're thrown in the deep end, you soon learn to swim!

Mary and Joe had not discussed any of the management details with us. 'You'll soon pick it up', was the sum of their advice. We established systems for controlling the house and the bars, simply by drawing on our own experience as hotel guests, and what I had learned in my working life stood me in good stead. It didn't take us long to find our way around the hotel industry.

The Windsor was a perfect example of suburban hotels of the time. It was the heartbeat of the small shopping precinct around it - affectionately known as 'the village'. Grocer, draper, pharmacist, bootmaker, hairdresser, barber, service station. What more could you need? Everyone knew everyone else, and the village had its own quota of identities and offbeat characters to set it apart from any other suburban centre.

In keeping with similar hotels, the Windsor relied on the bars for income and profit. The house section was maintained, simply because it was a provision of the licence that a minimum of eight rooms be kept available to the public and three standard meals be on offer daily in the hotel dining room. It was more or less accepted that it was impossible to make a profit from this side of the business, and you had done well if you 'broke even' in the final accounting at the end of the financial year. Small wonder the standard of board and lodging was low on the list of priorities in small suburban hotels.

Talk about new brooms sweeping clean! Within days we had identified a hundred reasons why the previous management should have been sent packing. The bars were Cole's domain. I concentrated my energies on the dining room, kitchen and guest rooms.

Curtains disintegrated in my hands as I took them down to be laundered. Only the undisturbed dust had kept them intact On an ancient Singer treadle machine, I made new window curtains and drapes for all sixteen bedrooms and, in the months ahead painted each and every room from ceiling to floor. Attractive old furniture had been smothered in layers of 'blackjack'; an obnoxious sticky substance used back then to cover marks and blemishes - a kind of lazy man's varnish. Liberal use of paint remover reclaimed the original timber and, by dint of much elbow grease and little cash, the bedrooms began to look quite appealing.

We gradually changed all the staff. I did not know it then, but soon learned, that 'inherited' members of staff are rarely successful. The last thing we wanted to hear was, 'but, we've always done it that way.'

Towards the end of the first week, Joe came over to see how things were going. He caught me fixing new green baize and white criss-crossed tape to what had been a shabby letter rack.

He seemed pleased. 'I can see you've got the right idea. Now we'd better settle your salary before you draw the wages cheque on Monday. The wife suggests £20 a week between you, £14 for Cole, £6 for you. Of course, your living expenses are included.' I knew this was generous and didn't even object to the inference that Cole would be doing more work than me. The reality proved to be quite the reverse! However, we were more than happy with the arrangement and felt our future was assured.

Needless to say, I made some mistakes in serving my apprenticeship with Mary Raine. When it came time to prepare the first month's accounts for payment I followed the instructions I had at Flower, Davies and Johnson - take off discounts where applicable and pay all creditors by the fifteenth of the month following date of invoice. I wrote the cheques and took them to Mary to be countersigned. She took a quick look.

'Goodness, my dear, what are you thinking of? If no discount is offered you don't pay the account until the last day of the following month. Now, send out only the payments that are discounted. Hold the others.' Mary lived by the maxim that if you looked after the pennies, the pounds would look after themselves.

It was one thing to get the bookwork right, another thing entirely to understand staff; to walk the fine line between getting them to do things your way, and having them storm off to the other job that was waiting round the corner. Mary didn't give me any advice on that particular juggling act.

Eileen, the housemaid, was an early problem. Noticing that she continued to ignore the clusters of cobwebs taking up residence in corners of the hallway, I introduced her - very gently, of course - to the cobweb broom. She looked at me as if she had been asked to do something utterly outrageous.

'I never look up Missus. No, I never look up. It would be the death of my back if I looked up.' Ah, well! I just added that one to the growing list of my own duties.

We had two sisters working for us - one as waitress, the other as kitchenmaid. They 'lived in', occupying two back rooms above a stairway leading down to the kitchen. The rear door of my office opened onto the foot of the stairs. After breakfast one morning I noticed both girls walking up to their rooms carrying laden trays. That's odd, I thought. My investigation revealed that 'breakfast in bed' was for boy friends who had stayed overnight! Of course, the girls should have been sacked on the spot, but such was the staffing problem that I read the riot act, but did not dismiss them.

It came as no surprise to discover soon afterwards that one of the girls was pregnant. Looking back I realise that in those days I was too idealistic for my own good. I decided it was my responsibility to look after her; she was a country girl and no parents seemed to be in the picture. I took her to the local doctor and enlisted his help in dealing with the dilemma. I assured her she could keep her job until she no longer wanted to work. The doctor arranged for her care when that time came and said he could find a family to adopt the baby if she so wished. The following week she was missing. Her sister claimed she was sick and staying with friends, but would be back in a couple of days. She was. Perky as ever, with the news that she had had an abortion.

'My mother always told me you'll never get a husband if you're called 'mum' before you're married.' Her mother should have told her considerably more than that!

Mary and Joe usually called in on Sunday mornings - part of their regular round trip to Fremantle to let the Austin stretch its legs. It was always a friendly and informal visit. Business matters were not discussed. Those waited until either Cole or myself called at the Wentworth on Monday.

The Wentworth made a feature of Christmas dinner and, when our first festive season was looming, we decided we should do something along the same lines. We felt sure Mary would like to see us do more to celebrate the occasion than had been done at the Windsor in the past. When the locals heard the village pub was 'doing' Christmas dinner, the dining room was booked out in no time. 'Booked out' meant we would have the grand total of ninety guests. With my limited experience it seemed like an enormous undertaking.

On Christmas Eve, I threw myself into the final preparations, decorating the dining-room with streamers stretched across the incredibly high ceiling; tables set with gleaming silver on white damask and all the appropriate festive touches. With orders already delivered to produce a perfect traditional menu, and extra staff hired, by the eve of the big day I felt I had done everything possible to ensure success. I began to relax and savour the special joy of Christmas.

Others had also relaxed. Notably the chef. His comings and goings into the saloon bar had not escaped Cole's attention. Because barmaids were paid at the same rate as men, bar workers were much easier to come by than domestic staff, so Cole had not needed to learn to temper his displeasure. He told the chef in no uncertain terms that, Christmas or no Christmas, he was not allowed to drink on duty. There was a heated exchange, clearly audible in my office. I sensed trouble. Within minutes Chef was at the door.

'OK. The boss says I can't have a drink on Christmas Eve. OK, so that's it then. If it's all right with you I'll snatch my time.'

I felt a rush of panic. 'Snatch my time'? What on earth was he saying, I asked myself. I'd never heard the expression before. Good grief! Was he telling me he wanted to leave? I hesitated for just one moment then, with all the authority I could muster, said firmly. 'No Chef. It's not all right with me. You know the rules. Please return to your work and we'll make it up to you after the meal is served tomorrow.' He turned quickly, leaving without a word. I sank into a chair in a relieved heap, the vision of ninety irate and unfed guests receding from my mind. I learned later that the words 'I'll snatch my time' were, as I feared, the vernacular term for giving notice.

It all went well on the day. That first Christmas we started a tradition which remained in place during the fourteen years the Windsor was our home. At the conclusion of the meal, we sat the staff down in the dining room and with the help of our permanent guests served them the same festive menu we had enjoyed, complete with wines and beer - and did the dishes and cleaning up afterwards!

We never stopped looking for new ways to increase turnover and to make our small hotel more popular. Cole came up with the idea of establishing a beer garden on the large area of grassed land which was part of the hotel property on the Suburban Road (now known as Mill Point Road) frontage. We set about planting buffalo runners in the worn sections of lawn and worked on the shrubs and gardens until the idea started to look like a real possibility.

We needed Mary's approval before investing in furniture for the venture. It was my job to prove to her that it was a good business proposition. She was hard to convince. Mary may have owned five city hotels and metropolitan properties too numerous to mention, but the possibility of reaping financial rewards from this beer garden idea was completely lost on her.

'How many tables and chairs do you want to buy?'

'A friend is helping Cole build the tables,' I replied. 'We thought we could start with forty-eight chairs.'

'Good heavens, my dear, what will you do with them all?'

When she finally agreed, I think it had more to do with rewarding my youthful enthusiasm than confidence in the success of the undertaking.

The beer garden had been open only a short time before we learned to expect more than two thousand people if the weather was hot. We would look down Mends Street towards the jetty as the ferries berthed, to watch the crowds spilling out of them and running up the hill to the Windsor. Yes, running. Forget the chairs. The rush was to secure a patch of grass to sit on!

Cole decided that the sensible way to serve beer to such large crowds was to use jugs. We stocked up on the regular water jugs which were standard on the tables of all hotel dining- rooms. Cole reasoned that the price of a jug of beer could be somewhat less than the going rate for the same quantity served in regular glasses. Volume of sales and speed of service would more than compensate for the reduced charge.

It was not long before a delegation from the United Licensed Victuallers Association - now known as the Australian Hotels Association - was on our doorstep, headed by the President, Mr Sid Johnston.

'You know, you cannot serve beer in containers other than those authorised by the Association. Anyway, you'll go broke if you continue to sell beer in jugs.'

It was a big mistake to tell Cole there was something he couldn't do, provided it was within the law - and we did not go broke. The rest, as they say, is history. Very soon every hotel in Perth was serving beer in jugs.

Author's collection

The author with Mary Raine, 1952

Live musical entertainment continued to be an important feature in the Wentworth lounge. We decided it would be an added attraction at the Windsor, particularly as music was not on offer at any of the other suburban hotels. We built a small bandstand in the garden, engaged musicians - pianist, violinist and cellist - and the Windsor Trio was born. Its popularity was immediate. The rush from the ferries intensified, and the locals complained about the influx of cars!

What else could we do to build on our success? By closing time on a busy night, happy crowds would be jigging and jiving on the lawns. Cole and I decided it was time to build a dance floor. There was a perfect spot for it in the middle of the garden where tall trees provided some measure of privacy. The crowds just got bigger.

Mary and Joe were very impressed when the beer garden venture proved to be such an outstanding success, and Mary did not hesitate to acknowledge that she had originally felt very sceptical about the idea.

Running the beer garden was a 'hands on' endeavour. Fortunately, it was seasonal, and we were ready for a let-up when the arrival of autumn announced an end to summer heat, prompting us to fix a date to close down for winter.

The beer garden continued to be an important part of our business and its popularity defied all competition during the years we were at the Windsor. We had pioneered the concept and we liked to think that we were not only the first, but also the best.

Our innovations proved their worth in the area that really matters to employers. At the end of the financial year following our appointment, the 'bottom line' showed we had tripled the previous year's net profit. We felt very pleased with ourselves, and Joe and Mary were pleasantly surprised.

The advent of New Australians went a long way towards easing staff shortages, and from time to time we availed ourselves of the new labour market. Among the first to work at the Windsor were Andrew and his wife, Marta. They were from Czechoslovakia and came to us as yardman and housemaid. Andrew, with his fresh good looks and hesitant charm, could have been any parent's favourite son. In his own country he had been a teacher, and his exquisite manners were evidence of a world far removed from the Windsor Hotel yard work. His educated politeness sometimes got him into trouble. Replying to a request from Kathy, our very Australian kitchenmaid, Andrew, as was his habit, bowed slightly from the waist and said. 'Your vishes to me is commands.' Kathy failed to interpret this as, 'Your wish is my command,' and the intended compliment was lost on her. She stormed into my office declaring angrily: 'That bloody New Australian says I'm vicious. That's it! I'm leavin'.'

Needless to say, I became awfully good at making the peace.

Then there was Panas. He was a yardman too. Panas was from Russia. A quiet, efficient little man who didn't talk much. He deplored untidiness and lived by the creed that there was a place for everything and everything should be in its place.

Cole was pretty casual about what he did with the tools after using them. When Panas found evidence of this he vented his exasperation in words that have become part of our own family joke lore. 'Do zee job - *five* minutes. Find zee tool - *twenty* minutes!'

Our Dutch barman, Wilhelm, convinced me that the Dutch are incredibly honest people. On one occasion he walked into the saloon bar from outside clutching a £5.0.0 note. He held it aloft and asked if anyone had lost it. Fifty Australian hands shot up!

They were happy times. I remember the New Australians who worked for us all those years ago with respect and affection. I have no doubt that many of them went on to write some wonderful pages in the Australian story.

From the time I first met Mary she suffered recurring bouts of pneumonia, and 1950 was a bad year. It was during one particularly severe attack that I realised just how devoted Joe was to his wife. He slept on a mattress beside their bed so that she had room to toss in comfort, whilst he was still close by should she need him during the night.

When Mary took ill, Joe asked me if I could spare a couple of hours in the afternoons to look after the lounge desk at the Wentworth. 'I hope I'm not asking too much, but you know how important the desk is to the wife. She just won't rest unless she knows it's in good hands.'

I quickly assured him that I could manage it. Mornings were my busy times. It was not a problem. Whilst supervising I also checked the current Wentworth invoices and prepared accounts for payment. When Mary recovered and was back to her normal routine it was decided she and Joe should rest every afternoon between 2.00 p.m. and 5.00 p.m., so the arrangement with me remained in place.

On 25 June 1950, it was reported that North Korea had suddenly invaded South Korea. The news had little impact even when the United Nations intervened under United States leadership. However, when Prime Minister Robert Menzies responded immediately by placing two Royal Australian Navy ships, the destroyer *Bataan* and the frigate *Shoalhaven*, at the disposal of the United Nations, there were anxious murmurings. Was this the start of World War III?

Australia was the first non-American nation to lend active support to the South Korean Army. Within days of the naval commitment the Government announced that Australia would provide a force of volunteers drawn from the permanent army and World War II veterans. With others, Mary and Joe wondered how it would all end.

Concern for Mary's health remained. She and Joe began to talk about taking a holiday - a real holiday, a trip back to England. He was delighted, especially when he got caught up in the detailed planning. For years he had dreamed of visiting his parents' homes in the old country, but had never been in the financial position to do so. He wanted to discover his roots and to unearth the family crest his father had talked about so often.

Bookings were made on the P & O liner *Australia*, departing from Fremantle on 7 July 1951, due back 2 November of the same year. The trip was timed to take advantage of the gap between the end of the financial year and the busy summer holiday and Christmas period.

It was arranged for Cole and me to take over the Wentworth during Mary and Joe's absence. Application for the transfer of the liquor licence was made, to date from the beginning of July. Cole's brother, Colin, a bachelor at the time, took over the licence at the Windsor and I was left with responsibility for the house section of both hotels. Writing about it now, I can see it was a huge undertaking, but at the time it seemed quite manageable. However, I do remember long days when I was positively aching with fatigue by bedtime.

Once Mary and Joe had made their bookings and preliminary planning was in place, there was a great deal of excitement and organising. It seemed natural for me to mention to Mary that she would probably need to make some additions to her wardrobe. I remember her reply.

'Not really. I've already bought two blouses and intend to get a handbag. I haven't had a new one since 1939.'

Mrs Boom told me she offered her services to make some dresses and skirts. When told 'no', she made the mistake of trying to be persuasive and got short shrift for her efforts.

This did not surprise me. Mary's personal wants were easily satisfied. The frugal habits born of necessity during the early years of her life stayed with her, and even when she was one of the wealthiest women in Perth, she lived as simply as when every shilling counted. The trappings of wealth and the display that so often accompanies it, held no charm for Mary. On one occasion she said to me.

'If you had a lot of money my dear, I guess you'd see all sorts of things you'd like to buy.'

I nodded my agreement.

'It's strange. I have no interest at all in buying things unless I can't do without them. I enjoy the challenge of making a success of an investment, but I lose sight of the money. It means nothing.'

In recent months, Mary had been called on to explain to the Taxation Department why the amount shown for personal drawings in her return was so unusually small; the inference being that hotel takings were being diverted for private use and not declared in full. Mary managed to convince the investigating officer that the incredibly small amount did, in fact, provide for all her needs.

As the date of departure drew closer, we had long discussions with Mary and Joe about the day-to-day running of the hotel. Quite naturally, Mary wanted to feel the business would continue just as if she was there herself. I was fortunate in having Mrs Boom as a backup. She was so familiar with procedures at the reception desk and in the dining room that I knew I could count on her to carry on in those departments while I concentrated on the office work, banking, ordering, staffing and general management. Cole's domain, encompassing the bars and drinking lounge, was the most difficult and demanding area.

Handing over inevitably involved a degree of tension, but there was still a happy air of expectancy about it. We were looking forward to taking up the new challenge, and I could see Mary and Joe were looking forward to putting routine behind them for a while.

Chapter 10

We want to retire

1951 - 1952

Mary and Joe timed their holiday to capture the best of the English summer. It was hoped the sea air during the voyage and mild warm days during their stay, would complete Mary's recovery from her most recent illness.

The trip was pleasantly uneventful. Joe settled into the shipboard routine of good eating and convivial drinking. He enjoyed meeting fellow passengers, and was doing what he enjoyed most when hosting pre-dinner get-togethers around the cocktail bar.

When Mary's family in England heard she was bringing her husband to meet them, there were no lack of invitations from relatives anxious to offer hospitality. However, Joe and Mary opted to stay at a small hotel in the heart of London.

Mary's niece, Beryl Hobson, remembers the visit.

> Aunt Birdie and Joe had been married for eight years but none of the family had met him. After they arrived there were lots of dinners with relatives - all eager to give Joe the once-over. I found him very affable and obviously anxious to please his wife, as well as to make a good impression on her family, However, I recall that even though family members were slow to warm to him, by the end of the visit most confessed that they liked him. There were early reservations about how genuine he was, and about his motives in marrying Birdie - after all he was thirteen years her junior. I suppose it was inevitable there would be prejudice against him, with the possibility of wealth by inheritance now becoming most unlikely! My personal impression was that he thought the world of his wife. He was certainly most attentive to her, and as a person, he could be very charming.[1]

Mary enjoyed showing Joe the traditional attractions of London - architectural landmarks and institutions he had only read about. However, Joe was conscious of his own English roots and lost no time in making arrangements to trace his family tree, and research the Raine crest. His objectives were surprisingly easy to achieve and he returned to Perth with a framed authenticated record of his ancestry. This hung in the foyer of the Wentworth for many years, and now graces the wall of the new owners' boardroom. Joe had the crest embossed on a gold ring which he wore until his death and which later came into the possession of his godson, Mark Yeldham Sangster.

Mary and Joe's visit coincided with the first large-scale trade exhibition held in England since the war. 'The Festival of Britain', mounted on the south bank of the Thames, was a showcase for the country's post war progress towards recovery in manufacturing, rural production, trade and commerce.[2] Mary and Joe spent several days there, absorbing the latest information and trade projections for the future. Mary in particular, had a lively interest in what was going on in the world and was very receptive to new ideas.

Although his wife 'phoned Perth almost daily - 'just to make sure there were no problems' - Joe could not help noticing how relaxed and happy she had become since leaving business concerns behind her. She was a different person. He would have been less than human not to wish this idyllic existence could continue - and why not? he asked himself. There was more money than they could use in a dozen lifetimes. Retirement was something he longed for, and the thought of living privately was a Utopian vision constantly at the back of his mind. Mary had not been receptive to the tentative suggestions he put forward in the past and he had become reluctant to broach the subject.

Unfortunately, even in this near-perfect situation, Mary had days when she was not well enough to leave their room. Joe thought more and more about the wisdom of retiring.

Over the years Mary had sponsored all but three of her siblings to join her in Western Australia. Those remaining in England were

Charles (Charlie), her eldest brother, Laura Cooke and Elsie Norchi, her youngest sisters. They and their families were first on Mary and Joe's visiting list.

Charlie and his wife, Ivy, had not fared as well financially as family members who joined Mary in Western Australia. Charlie had followed the lead of his maternal grandparents, going into a retail venture supplying fish and poultry. Not having the entrepreneurial drive of his eldest sister, he was content to pursue this calling until retirement, by which time supermarkets had started to put small shops out of business. When ill-health began to take its toll, Mary responded to a plea for monetary assistance.[3]

Elsie was a great favourite with Mary. They enjoyed a common interest, investing in the share market, and Mary left a portfolio with Elsie to trade at her own discretion. Letters from her to her sister reported on successful selling and investing.

Among Mary's personal letters was one from Elsie remembering the visit.

> I shall always picture you and Joe at No 7 Hillside, and recall the happy times we all spent together despite the bouts of sickness you had. I so well remember the day we saw you off at Dover, saying goodbye and feeling so sad and lonely after you had gone.[4]

On many occasions Mary had tried to bring her second youngest sister, Laura (Lolly) Cooke, to Perth. She was determined that during this visit she would make one more effort. Lolly's daughter, Mary's niece Beryl Hobson, recalls her mother's own words in speaking about her sister.

> As a child I was always rather scared of Birdie - especially when she was left in charge of us during our mother's absence.
> Our father was inclined to over-indulge at the local inn, and at these times could become quite abusive. Our mother would leave the house and go to stay with her sister until he calmed down! He suffered from bad migraine too, and that didn't improve his temper.
> Birdie was almost a second mother to her younger brothers and sisters. Being the eldest, she was very responsible, and when I look back I can see that a lot was expected of her. She wouldn't put up with any nonsense. I remember one occasion when she

was brushing my long thick hair; I made such a fuss when she tried to get the tangles out of it, she grabbed the scissors and cut it all off!

Birdie was always busy. As well as working in our father's shops and training as a pupil-teacher, she sewed for all of us, and quite often would fall asleep with her head on the sewing machine.

When Birdie came home to see us in 1922, she borrowed a car and drove some of us around with her. My sister Elsie, the youngest, was a keen swimmer and kept begging to be taken to the sea. When we finally reached the coast, Birdie stopped the car and proclaimed in exasperation. 'There's your bloody sea - now go and look at it!'

During this visit my husband was very ill with pneumonia. Birdie suggested that we should emigrate to Western Australia with our three daughters, as the climate there would be so much better for him. It didn't happen, because Herbert had started his own business and didn't want to leave England.

He died of tuberculosis just five years later and Birdie tried again to get us out to Perth, but arrangements were in place for our second daughter, Beryl, to go to the Masonic School as a boarder, so the offer was refused.

In 1939, Birdie suggested yet again that we join her in Western Australia, but Beryl was now nineteen and eligible for war service. She couldn't leave the country and, of course, I wouldn't leave without her, although my youngest daughter, Audrey, and I could have left.

I thought Birdie would have given up on me, but when she brought Joe to meet us in 1951, she repeated the offer and I came back to Perth with them.

She was a wonderful sister, and although I was rather in awe of her at this stage of our lives, I loved her dearly.[5]

Beryl Hobson added her own memories of her aunt.

Aunt Birdie had an incredibly strong sense of family. After all the failed attempts to get my mother and her family to Perth, when her sister was widowed, Aunt Birdie did not hesitate to take her back to Perth and to offer her a home at the Wentworth for life.

At the time of the visit with Joe, plans were already in place for my husband and me and our two sons, to emigrate to Perth under Aunt Birdie's sponsorship. We arrived in 1952 after a full year's delay from the time of making the decision to actually getting here.

We stayed at the Wentworth for more than two months, at which

> time Aunt Birdie offered to sell us a home she owned in Melville Parade, South Perth. It was tenanted by a lady who cried and made such a fuss when asked to leave, that my aunt, renowned for her toughness, caved in and decided we should find another place. She guaranteed our loan from the bank when we purchased a home in Labouchere Road, South Perth. We always remembered the property in Melville Parade with gnawing regret, as it was in a wonderful position and was subsequently worth a lot of money.
>
> My mother was a gentle, quiet woman, a total contrast to her sister, Aunt Birdie. In fact, the Carter family were such a mixed lot - no two were alike in that family - that it was hard to believe they all had the same mother and father. The genes got well and truly distributed!
>
> My Aunt Birdie was single-minded about everything she did and once she made a decision it was next to impossible to shift her from it. She worked incredibly hard, but seemed to enjoy the regime she set herself. Aunt Birdie had a wonderful sense of humour and a great talent for telling the stories of her early years in Australia.
>
> Although my aunt was not given to outward displays of warmth, even within her close family, she could be generous to a fault if moved by some special circumstance. She was truly of a special breed, and I remember her with genuine affection.[6]

For Joe, the holiday ended all too soon. For Mary, once she turned for home, she couldn't get there quickly enough. The *Australia* berthed at Fremantle wharf early on the morning of 2 November. Cole was there to meet them and the new arrival, Lolly.

Within an hour of walking into the hotel foyer, Mary was in full flight, taking up the reins at the Wentworth as if she had just returned from a quick visit to the shops.

For my part I was very happy to hand over the contents of the safe to Joe, give Mary an update on what had been happening and escape to the relative calm of running the Windsor. Cole was probably more relieved than I was to shed the responsibility for the Wentworth, as controlling and supervising the lounge was an aspect of the work that did not appeal to him. There had been no major problems during the owners' absence and it was a good feeling to know we had done our job well.

Returning to the Windsor, we faced the busiest time of our year, with the beer garden due to open in a few weeks' time. It had become my winter hobby to brighten the outdoor furniture with a fresh coat of paint in readiness for the new season's business. Needless to say, this had gone by the board whilst I shared my energies between the demands of running two hotels. Hastening to make up for lost time, I set up shop in a small area behind my office adjacent to the saloon bar. Directly above my workplace, on the outside wall, was an early model evaporative air conditioner which made a token effort to make it more inviting to be inside the bar than out. A trickle of fluid dripped from its overflow pipe. It was a sweltering day - a century on the old scale - but nothing would stop me from working to plan.

Late that evening I was overwhelmed by a headache unlike anything I had ever experienced in my life. It was accompanied by a raging fever. The local doctor ordered my immediate transfer to hospital - 'by ambulance, not car'. I remained in hospital for eight weeks, the first two fighting for my life against a form of viral pneumonia that defied all tests to identify it. I have since wondered if it could have been a strain of Legionnaire's Disease - unheard of in 1951.

Joe and Mary were regular visitors and, I learned later, were very concerned about me in the early days of my illness, even going so far as to make plans to bring my parents over from Newcastle. It is probably fortunate that I was never aware of how gravely ill I was. A strong constitution prevailed and I gradually regained my normal good health and boundless energy.

The drama of my sudden illness is probably the reason why I did not know I had inadvertently incurred Mary's displeasure.

One of my projects during our custodianship at the Wentworth had been to smarten up the dining room, with attention to the standard of staffing as well as service. This involved new uniforms and a more varied menu. Mary was not pleased to find that changes had been made during her absence. Now I am older and wiser, I realise what I did was ill-considered and I should have known better. It was a case of enthusiasm overriding common sense. However, whatever antagonism Mary may have felt towards me evaporated immediately she heard I was ill. She never mentioned the matter and I would have remained in ignorance of this small hiccup in our relationship had Joe not told me about it a long time afterwards.

Subsequent events suggest that Mary was quick to forgive and forget.

It was April 1952. We were thinking about setting a date to close the beer garden season.

Joe 'phoned asking us to call over next day. It was not an unusual request. There was often some aspect of the management to be discussed. However, what they wanted to talk about really caught us on the hop.

Mary spoke first.

'Joe is anxious to retire and we have decided to live privately. Now - we want you to lease the Wentworth from us.'

My face must have mirrored my dismay and the thoughts running riot in my head. How could they possibly imagine we had the kind of money it would take to buy the lease of a hotel like the Wentworth? We couldn't pay the ingoing, let alone purchase the furniture, plant and fittings for a huge business with almost seventy bedrooms.

Mary must have sensed what was going through my mind and didn't wait for me to speak. 'This will be a special lease. We have decided to leave the Wentworth. That is quite definite, and we want you to take it over. Financially, we will make it as easy as possible for you.'

Joe broke in: 'The fact is, we could place the hotel under management, but then the wife would be here every day watching what was going on. There would be no point in us leaving. We have already had a word with Parker and Parker, our solicitors, and they are working out a leasing agreement. They warn us it will be complicated. It will be along these lines. You will pay no upfront ingoing. You don't have to purchase the furniture, plant and fittings as would be required under a normal leasing agreement. There will be a monthly payment, a kind of rental that will include the proportion of ingoing plus a monthly hire fee for the furniture, plant and fittings. You can rest assured that, whatever charges are fixed, you will make good money for your efforts. It would be pointless for us to ask you to pay beyond what would leave you with worthwhile profits. Now, what do you say?'

We were both in shock, but somehow stuttered out a feeble 'Yes,' then went home to consider the implications of what we had agreed to. We knew it wasn't going to be easy, but it was the opportunity of a lifetime and we'd be foolish to pass it up.

We soon learned Mary and Joe had already done more towards their retirement plan than brief Parker and Parker to prepare the unusual leasing agreement.

On 14 March 1949, they had bought a large home on the corner of Mary and Preston Streets, Como. The vendor was the University of Western Australia. It is interesting that the next time the property changed hands it returned to the University. Today the land it occupied is part of a South Perth Motel complex.

The home was exceptionally large and had at one time been used as a school, then subsequently divided into two separate residences, one being occupied by Mary's sister Toby and her husband Bill, the other tenanted. Mary and Joe saw it as an ideal home in which to retire. It was in a quiet suburb, close, but not too close to the city, and large enough for two people who were used to having plenty of room around them. Joe's bulk and stature demanded space and Mary was used to ranging the corridors of a large hotel. They would have felt caged in the sort of home any other two people on their own, might consider suitable. They intended to make a few improvements, but major alterations were not necessary. There would be no need for Toby and Bill to move.

Suddenly, there was so much to do that just thinking about it sent me into a fever of self-doubt. In ten weeks' time we were taking on the biggest challenge we had ever tackled. We wanted to leave everything at the Windsor in good shape for Cole's brother Colin, who was taking over the management. The situation created a wonderful opportunity for him and he was understandably pleased at this unexpected chance to run a hotel.

The State Licensing Court met only quarterly, and the licence of the Wentworth had only returned to Joe from Cole in January that year. Now, within months, the situation had to be reversed. Joe undertook to attend to that formality.

We would have liked to take a holiday before embarking on our new enterprise. It was only three months since I had left hospital, seriously underweight and probably needing a longer convalescence, but Mary and Joe were set on making 30 June their retirement date, and it was not possible for us to be absent in the short time remaining. We put holiday plans out of our minds.

Early in May, we met with Mary and Joe and a solicitor from Parker and Parker to sign the lease, which the firm's representative described as 'one of the most complicated hotel leasing agreements we have ever prepared.' I wouldn't doubt it for a moment. The volume of the document certainly supported the claim. With the signing we knew the die was cast.

There were a lot more visits to the Wentworth and long discussions as we worked towards ensuring a smooth changeover. It came as no surprise to receive a call from Joe during the first week in June.

'Can you both come over? Make it soon. Something urgent has cropped up.' We agreed to call in the following morning.

We went early and found Joe alone in his office. After an unusually subdued greeting, he hesitated before answering our unspoken question.

'I don't quite know how to tell you this. The truth is - the wife doesn't want to leave the Wentworth. Now the time is getting close, she can't bear the thought of living anywhere else. With the papers signed and everything else, I hardly know what to say.' His voice trailed away.

There was a moment's silence before I spoke. ‘It doesn’t matter. Mrs Raine doesn’t have to go.’

Cole broke in: ‘Tear up the lease. It’s OK. I’ve wondered if Mrs Raine would be able to do it when the time came.’

Joe smiled with relief. ‘Rainee and I have talked about this, and we are going to make it up to you by giving you a lease of the Windsor. Normally, we wouldn’t even consider leasing that hotel.’ It was our turn to smile. A lease of the Windsor was what we would have chosen above the Wentworth, or any other hotel for that matter. We went home bursting with excitement at the unexpected turn of events.

The most disappointed party to all the planning had to be Joe. He came so close to realising his dream of living in retirement, now it was denied him. It was not to be. A measure of his true love for Mary was that he never made a murmur of recrimination or even voiced his disappointment. They settled back into their accepted way of life and the question of retirement was never raised again.

The generous special terms Mary and Joe had given us to lease the Wentworth did not transfer to the offer on the Windsor. It was a regular hotel leasing agreement but, of course, there was a vast difference in the sums of money required. I was fortunate in having a father who was prepared to guarantee the loan we needed from the Commonwealth Bank. Cole and I couldn’t have been happier. To have a lease of the Windsor was a dream come true. We could shed the restrictions of being managers for the independence of being lessees. Now we could start the family we had waited for.

Chapter 11

So dearly loved. So sadly missed

1952 - 1957

The Korean war ended with the signing of a truce on 27 July 1953. The jubilation in Seoul was not evident in Perth, although the end of hostilities brought a collective sigh of relief.

The Wentworth lounge was a magnet for Australian servicemen returning to their home States via Perth. Understandably, they were in high spirits, with grim memories behind them and the prospect of family reunions ahead.

The high spirits frequently got out of hand, sometimes ending in scenes reminiscent of World War II. Mary and Joe had worked hard to rid the Wentworth of this image of badly behaved servicemen and they were not prepared to allow what had been achieved to be undone. After a spate of unpleasant incidents, Joe thought he had found the answer when he put up a notice in the lounge, which read.

> After 6.00 p.m. men in uniform who are not accompanied by female companions, will be served in the bars.

The notice caused more problems than it solved. The State President of the Returned Servicemen's League (Mr F C Chaney) described the ban as 'unjust and unfair.' Joe defended the decision by reminding his critics that the hotel had been placed 'out of bounds' to Australian servicemen during World War II because of similar behaviour, and he was trying to pre-empt a repetition of the ban. Nonetheless, he responded to the objections and removed the notice almost immediately.

The last thing Joe wanted was to get caught up in any kind of unpleasantness. He and Mary liked to live quietly these days. After the abortive attempt to retire, Mary realised that she owed it to Joe to make some changes in their lifestyle. They spent more time with family and took regular nights off to see a movie or attend live shows which were on in Perth. On those occasions when she preferred to stay at home, Mary encouraged Joe to go out, often with hotel guests.

Joe never lost his love of the outdoors, but it was difficult to reconcile this with hotel living. Nonetheless, he did find a way to enjoy the satisfaction of coaxing growth from damp cool earth. He started cultivating mushrooms in the hotel cellars. From unexciting beginnings, his crops got better and better. He loved to brag about his success and give samples to his friends.

There were also changes in Mary's business life. Although she still found the same satisfaction in running her beloved Wentworth, she had lost her zest for acquiring new properties, declaring herself content with what she already owned.

Sometime in the middle of July, I found Joe sitting quietly in his office and decided it was a good time to surprise him with the news that Cole and I were expecting our first child in late November.

'Ah! I knew it. I told Rainee just last week I thought you were pregnant. Well. That's marvellous. It will be a boy of course, and what's more, I'm going to be his godfather.'

I hadn't even considered the matter, but hastened to assure Joe that I couldn't think of anyone we would rather have, then lost no time in asking Mary if she would share the obligation and be our baby's godmother.

They couldn't have been more excited if I had been their own daughter.

Mark Yeldham Sangster was born to a welcoming world on 24 November 1953, a strong, healthy baby. Mary and Joe shared our joy on the birth of a much-wanted son, and Joe immediately took steps to enrol the new arrival at his old school, Guildford Grammar. He was bitterly disappointed when advised that only sons, and not godsons, were eligible for preferred enrolment, and there were no other vacancies.

Author's collection

Day of Mark's christening 31st January 1954

The prospective godparents were duly advised that the Christening service would be held at St Mary's Anglican Church in South Perth at 3.00 p.m. on Sunday 31 January 1954.

Mary had not been well in the weeks since Christmas, and when the weather forecast warned of a scorching day, we were afraid she might not be able to attend the ceremony. We need not have worried. She insisted it was an event she would not miss.

After the service we celebrated the occasion in the Windsor garden with a gathering of family and friends, taking photographs of Mary and Joe in a role that was certainly foreign to them. Their gift to Mark was a silver christening mug, and a bank account with £10 in it. Joe explained that each birthday this would grow by the same amount multiplied by Mark's age, until he turned 21.

Mary's health was always cause for concern. Martie Sundstrum of Melville recalls relieving as Mary Raine's private nurse at the end of 1953, after what she understood was a very serious illness. Martie remembers the 'big man' downstairs who seemed to run everything.[1]

Of course, the big man was Joe, who enjoyed excellent health. I cannot remember him ever being sufficiently unwell to spend a day in bed. He was a heavy smoker, but in those days cigarette smoking was so much a part of life it meant nothing whether you smoked two a day or two packets a day. There was never a suggestion that smoking carried a health risk, either to smokers or to those around them. Hotel lounges and bars were, for most of the time, veiled in a gauzy white fog, and emptying ashtrays was almost as important as serving drinks. Cigarette smoke, along with loud laughter and noisy chatter was part of the ambience that created the appeal of these public places. It is hard to imagine anything as obnoxious as the smokers' spittoons beneath the footrail of almost all bars, yet they were accepted as normal accessories.

Today, Mary's recurring lung-related illnesses would be linked immediately to the environment in which she spent her life, but in the 1950s, awareness of the danger of smoking was a long way off.

One of Mrs Boom's daughters, Ethel Allen, and her husband, Harry, remember when, in 1954, they succeeded in getting Mary to agree to Joe going with them on a holiday to Melbourne.

> We had mentioned to Joe that we were going to Melbourne on the *Menora*, one of the State ships that cruised regularly between Perth and Sydney. He was almost joking when he said: 'Can I come too?' One thing led to another, and because Mary was enjoying a rare period of better health, she agreed she could manage without Joe for a week or two. He lost no time in booking a cabin.
>
> Joe had the time of his life on board that ship. He really let his hair down. He loved people, and he loved being the centre of attention. Every evening he entertained fellow passengers in his cabin, turning on pre-dinner drinks from the cases of spirits and liqueurs he had brought on board with him. You can imagine how popular he was! Because it was often hard to get proper liqueur glasses, he had brought a quantity of small medicine glasses, and we laughed every time he put them out.
>
> Joe stayed at the Victoria Hotel in Elizabeth Street, and when we were not able to pick him up, he took taxis to get around and see all the places of interest. Harry's family took him out to dinner at all the special restaurants. Joe was in his element.
>
> He returned to Perth by plane, leaving quite some time before us. His 'leave pass' had expired.[2]

The arrival of our son meant we saw more of Joe than in the past. He would call in briefly any time he and the Austin happened to be south of the river. Joe took his role of godfather very seriously, and considered it part of his duties to keep abreast of the baby's progress.

Business at the Windsor continued to grow, but we could see there was still significant untapped potential. The problem was that major structural changes needed to be made before it would be possible to cater for more customers. As lessees, we made some cosmetic alterations, such as relocating the lounge service hatch from the back of the front bar to the side of the saloon bar, giving a privacy that had been lacking for those seated or buying drinks. The project included repainting and recarpeting.

We also built a solid, rendered, dwarf wall to the ground floor at street level. This separated the verandah from the footpath and, with the addition of tables and chairs, provided an interesting outdoor drinking area. It is now usual for verandahs and balconies of licensed premises to be used in this way, but it was considered very 'new' back then. The area remains unchanged today. These improvements had required approval from Mary and Joe, but no financial input from them.

We were waiting for the right time to discuss the subject of rebuilding the beer garden service area to include a cold room where kegs could be put on a multi-coupling system. Remembering the volume of beer sold, it was amazing we had managed with the old-fashioned method of hoisting kilderkins from the front cellar, to be used some fifteen metres away.

I had just put Mark to bed one evening in late 1954, when Joe arrived unexpectedly.

The warm greeting was followed by my usual suggestion.

'Can I get you a beer?'

'Yes. Why not? Just happened to be passing.'

I could tell there was something on Joe's mind. He accepted the beer, and looked at me as if waiting to judge a reaction. 'Today we had an offer from someone who wants to buy the Windsor.' My heart sank. I struggled to retain my composure. Joe didn't embarrass me by waiting for a comment. 'Now, don't look so worried. We aren't going to sell; but it's a lot of money - £100,000. I admit we were tempted, and I think the agent would have offered more had we shown any real interest, but the wife said "No," and that was the end of it.'

Cole and I talked about this later, and decided it was not a good time to ask Mary and Joe to spend money on alterations or additions.

The incident made me realise how much I loved the small hotel, and how hard it would be to leave it.

Mary and Joe had many calls on their generosity and were regularly targeted by organisations in need of funds. They could not respond to every request, but a certain number were always answered. When an appeal was launched by the University of

Western Australia to raise funds for a Medical School, a direct approach was made to Mary and Joe. Mary was not available on the day of the meeting, and Joe was alone when he spoke with fundraisers from the University. He became convinced that the establishment of a Medical School was a wonderful objective. He wanted to become involved as a major donor, inferring that the donation from Mary and himself would be substantial. When he talked the matter over with his wife, the sum agreed on was less than he had hoped to give. Joe was disappointed, but Mary promised they would donate again in the near future.

A hotel regular who was a distributor for MGM films, mentioned to Cole that it was now possible to hire many of the old movies, together with a projector and screen. It became routine to invite family and hotel guests to join us in the coffee lounge on Sunday evenings to watch a show. We often invited Mary and Joe and they enjoyed the company as well as the entertainment.

It was entirely lawful, but sometimes the level of noise and laughter had Cole saying: 'Better tone it down a bit everyone. The lounge is noisier than when we're open for business.'

In early 1956, hotels in the eastern suburbs were being systematically targeted by thieves, offices raided, and safes which would not yield their contents, physically removed. The culprits successfully thwarted all efforts to catch them.

We were surprised to receive a visit from a police officer.

'We've heard a whisper that the Windsor, Como and Hurlingham Hotels will be the next hit by these thieves who are giving us the run-around. We want to station some of our men inside the hotel and with a bit of luck we'll catch them red-handed. Mind if we take a look at the place?'

Cole nodded assent and asked: 'When are you going to do this?'

'I can't answer that right now. Sometimes we get a tip-off. Sometimes we act on a hunch. It could be any time. What's important is that you know what's going on.'

A few weeks later we were enjoying a movie in the coffee lounge with Mary, Joe and others, when there was an incessant banging at the front door. Cole rushed to open it as I realised there was also loud knocking at the rear door. I hurried in that direction. Uniformed police moved into the foyer from both directions, with Cole and me caught in the middle.

Cole was friendly. 'Good to see you. I thought you would have let us know, but it doesn't matter. So, you think something might happen tonight? Where are you going to hide? There's an ideal place in the stairwell opposite the office door.'

The four officers looked a bit nonplussed. The younger men turned to the sergeant, waiting for him to respond to Cole's familiar greeting. The sergeant seemed to be groping for words.

'See here, Mr Sangster, we've had a written complaint that this hotel has been unlawfully trading on Sunday evenings for the past month. Noise can be heard from outside and I need to check your drinking lounge.'

It was Cole's turn to look nonplussed. 'What's going on here? That's my family and our personal friends in the lounge. We're watching a movie. Aren't you here to set a trap for the safe robbers?'

By this time Joe and Mary had emerged to see what all the fuss was about, but their questions just added to the confusion. It took a while, but the comedy of errors was eventually sorted out. The unexpected callers were from the Liquor Branch and the callers we were expecting were from the Criminal Investigation Branch. We were assured that neither branch knew about the other's operation. The incident was more entertaining than the movie and Mary was highly amused.

In September 1956, Joe called in with a plan he had drawn up. It was for a cold room to be built next to the beer garden service bar. He had obviously recognised the need before we mentioned it, and had spent a lot of time working out the most efficient way to set it up. The layout showed locations for ten kilderkins, with temprites and multi-coupling pipes, and provision for a large quantity of bottled beer. It was just what we wanted. Joe promised it would be ready for the summer trade.

Little did we know this was the last time we would see our dear friend in good health.

Within days of Joe's visit, I received an early morning 'phone call from Mrs Florence Isgar, a senior member of the Wentworth staff who worked on the reception desk. She broke the disturbing news that Joe had suffered a severe stroke the previous evening, and was in St John of God Hospital in Subiaco.

We hurried to the Wentworth to support Mary, then later to the hospital to see Joe. The news was not good. Joe was paralysed and had lost his power of speech. He could understand what was being said and could respond by moving his left hand or nodding his head. It was too early to say if there was hope for recovery, but the next twenty four hours would be crucial.

Mary was inconsolable. During those first painfully long twenty-four hours, she barely left his side, but sat holding his hand, murmuring his name, refusing to accept the possibility that he might not recover.

When the hours stretched into days without any sign of improvement, Mary was desperate. She pleaded with the doctors.

'Why can't you do something for Joe? Is there a specialist in the eastern States? Surely there's a doctor somewhere in the world who can treat him? I don't care what it costs. You must do something.'

The reply was always the same.

'I am sorry Mrs Raine, but your husband has had a severe stroke, the result of arteriosclerosis. The causes of the condition are not fully understood and there is nothing we can do to treat him. We can only wait and see if he regains his speech and mobility.'

The doctors could give Mary no prognosis. The days stretched into weeks, but there was no real improvement in Joe's condition. It was decided he would be more comfortable in his own home.

A hospital bed was installed in room seven, which had been our home when we lived at the Wentworth. Mary engaged a team of nurses to look after Joe around the clock. Even then, she did not give up hope, but spent hours massaging his hands, arms and legs as if her will could return the vigour he had lost. She talked to him constantly, waiting for a sign that he understood what she was saying, bolstering her hopes as she imagined that today he held her hand more firmly, or moved his head more strongly.

We were constant callers, as were many of Joe's friends - reluctant to admit, even to ourselves, that each visit could be the last.

On 11 February 1957, Joe was rushed to St John of God Hospital. He had suffered a severe cerebral haemorrhage and died soon after. He was buried in the Anglican grassed area of Karrakatta Cemetery on 14 February. The funeral was well attended by family and friends, as well as representatives from the liquor industry and various business houses.

It was cruel to witness Mary's anguish.

The headstone Mary chose for Joe's final resting place read.

So dearly loved. So sadly missed.

Chapter 12

The long day closes

1957 - 1960

What happens when you have no reason to go on living?

Mary asked herself this question when she returned to the Wentworth from Joe's funeral. For the first time she realised this place she called home was big, too big. Without Joe's comings and goings she felt lost in it. How could she go on without him? Could she go on without him?

It didn't help that she should have been prepared to lose him. Against all warnings, she had kept hoping for a miracle. Now it was over.

Mary retreated to the room they had shared for fourteen years. Joe's presence was real. She opened the lowboy, displaying neat layers of white underwear, and the conservatively coloured socks he favoured. She moved to the wardrobe where his suits hung waiting, then glimpsed the navy cashmere cardigan. He had bought it when they were in London in 1951. Mary remembered it was ridiculously expensive, but Joe wanted it, and against all sane thinking she encouraged him to buy it The handle of the small utility drawer of his bedside table responded to her touch, revealing handkerchiefs, cuff links, tie pins, name tags from functions long past, invitations never accepted, and there, pushed to the farthest corner, a bundle of letters secured by an elastic band. Mary realised they were the letters she had sent Joe during his rare absences in the years of their marriage. He had kept them all.

Memories flooded back and Mary found herself shaking with sobs. She fell against the bed. Grief, kept hidden in the chapel and at the graveside, welled up inside her, bursting in an uncontrollable torrent of scalding tears. She had no idea how long she wept, but when the flood was finally over, she felt release as from physical pain.

Mary knew she would weep silently for Joe until the day she died, but this had been her final, painful 'goodbye'. Life had to go on. She threw herself into work at the Wentworth, hoping the busy daily round would keep her mind off her loss.

Mrs Boom was a wonderful support. During the long weeks of Joe's illness, she had quietly taken over the duties Mary could no longer manage, and made sure general efficiency did not suffer because the boss was not on hand every day. Mrs Boom also realised Mary would need more personal help than in the past and, on the Sunday following Joe's funeral, asked her if she would like to visit the grave.

'Les will drive you if you'd like to go down to Karrakatta Cemetery. Should I order flowers?'

Les Brown was married to Mrs Boom's daughter, Hilda. Hilda remembers Mary as a likable and friendly person.

> Mrs Raine had a great sense of humour and she'd chuckle loudly when something was said that amused her. She wasn't an employer who gave gifts or bonuses. I can't remember Mum ever receiving a present of any kind, even at Christmas, but if you asked Mrs Raine for substantial help, she was quite likely to give it. We discovered this ourselves, when Les and I got married in 1953. We found a home we wanted to buy in Monash Avenue, South Perth. It cost four thousand pounds, but the bank wouldn't lend us the money without a guarantor. Mrs Raine didn't hesitate when we asked her to back us, but straight away she wanted something in return.
> 'You've got so much land here, my dear. How about fencing off a run at the back where we can raise turkeys for the hotel?' What could I say? I could hardly refuse. Soon after we moved in, Jacko, the yardman from the hotel, arrived with a clutch of turkey chicks, and set them up in their new home. He came regularly with scraps from the kitchen and when the birds were old enough took care of dispatching them for the Wentworth table.[1]

The Sunday drive became a ritual and Mary would not allow anything to interfere with it. Early in the morning Les would catch the bus from South Perth to the city, collect Joe's Austin A40 from the garage at the rear of the Wentworth, and call for Mary at about 10.00 a.m.

After visiting the graveside at Karrakatta, they made the round trip to Fremantle, then back to town. After lunch the routine was repeated, but this time the drive took them around Mounts Bay Road to the Swan Brewery building. Here they parked on the river verge and Mary insisted on listening to a regular Sunday sermon by Martin Luther King. Sometimes Hilda and Mrs Boom went with them and the party continued on to the Windsor Hotel for afternoon tea. At the end of the day, Les returned the car to the hotel and caught a bus back to his home.[2]

Though little was made of it at the time, Mary appreciated this kindness, and said 'thank you' in the best possible way. She left instructions that the car was to be given to Les and Hilda on her death.[3]

Mary had never considered for a moment that she could outlive Joe. Once, during a heart-to-heart talk with Paddy Baker, he had warned her of the possibility, and she was quite amused, reminding him that Joe was thirteen years her junior and enjoyed robust good health.

Paddy persisted. 'Joe is overweight, and he has the appetite of a growing boy. He's a man living out of his natural element too. Joe's meant to be out of doors, not closed in by walls and climbing up and down stairs to the cellar a dozen times a day. You think about it.'[4]

Paddy had been right, but it was all too late to think about it now. Mary knew it was time to accept her own mortality and decide what to do with her assets, and those that had now returned to her from Joe's estate.

Following their marriage, and the agreement to run the businesses as joint partners, Mary and Joe had made reciprocal wills.

Mary knew Joe intended to honour his promise to the University of Western Australia, to contribute a substantial sum towards the foundation of a Medical School. Sadly, he was not given time to make this provision in his will, although the project was very dear to his heart. During Joe's illness Mary became aware of how dependent medical research was on funding. There was so much still to be learned, but without funding, progress was slow towards solving medical questions that remained unanswered. Mary realised she could make good Joe's intention to help advance medical knowledge. She decided to renounce her interest in his will in favour of the University and a Medical Research Foundation.

Mary engaged solicitor Ken Hatfield, later a leading Queen's Council, to confer with the then Vice-Chancellor of the University, Stanley (later Sir Stanley) Prescott and representatives from the medical profession. The aim of the discussion was to arrange a deed of trust, whereby Joe's estate would pass to the University for the establishment of the Raine Research Foundation. This was completed in late February 1957.

Albert Hawke (uncle of Bob Hawke) was Premier of Western Australia at the time. When approached, he recognised the special importance of the Research Foundation and agreed to forego the £50,000 State probate on Joe's estate, provided the Commonwealth Government did likewise.

The then Chancellor of the University, Sir Alexander Reid, was a member of the Commonwealth Grants Commission. He successfully approached Robert Menzies, then Prime Minister of Australia, and the arrangement was in place.

As time went on, Mary relied more and more on help from the University, which now held a half interest in all her properties.

Mary was tired. Scarcely a day passed when she did not feel too ill to go on. She could see no purpose in her life. The question of what to do with the remaining share of her properties was never far from her thoughts. Two things became fixed in her mind. First, the wealth she had worked a lifetime to amass must remain intact.

Courtesy The West Australian

Mary Raine 1957

Secondly, it must, in some way, be used to investigate the cause and treatment of the disease that took Joe from her.

Arthur Valentine (Val) Abbott, Mary's solicitor, trusted friend and adviser for many years and a patron of the arts, urged Mary to consider endowing an art gallery. This was just one of many similar requests. Paddy Baker told me that she discussed most of them with him.[5]

'Paddy, everyone is telling me what I should, or should not do with my money. I want it to be used to find a cure for the disease that killed Joe. Those awful words: "There is nothing we can do," haunt me every day I live.'

Paddy encouraged her in her own conviction that she could do nothing more worthwhile with her estate than direct it, and the money it could generate, towards finding a cure for arteriosclerosis.

Mid-way through 1957, I was surprised to receive a call from Mary.

'Can you come over this afternoon, my dear?'

It was several weeks since I had occasion to call at the Wentworth. The atmosphere was more formal now the University had a representative working full time in the office. We frequently saw Mary on Sunday afternoons and relied on this contact to keep in touch.

Mary's appearance startled me. Seated behind the desk she had once dominated, and which was now much too large for her bent, gaunt frame, she looked so frail. Fine white hair, cut short as always, framed a face etched with lines of sorrow. The once piercing blue-grey eyes were dull and lifeless. I wanted to put my arms around her and murmur words of love and comfort, but something held me back.

Mary was shelling peas into a basin, hands out of sight beneath the top of the high lounge desk. I had seen her doing it hundreds of times; her way of saving the kitchen staff some time when they came on duty. In the past, I was amused, but today, I felt incredibly saddened. Mary looked up as she saw me coming.

'Hello, my dear.'

Mary never wasted time with pleasantries.

'I asked you to come over so I could tell you this myself. I have decided to leave almost all I own to the University to establish a Medical Research Foundation.

'Val Abbott wanted me to endow an art gallery. I almost agreed. But honestly, what's the point? Joe and I have never been interested in art. No. I have made up my mind. I've already done a lot for my family, and apart from two of my sisters and three of my grandnieces, I am leaving them nothing. There will be a few other bequests, but they are small. With Joe's estate, the total will generate substantial research funds.

'Now, about you and Cole. We have always been fond of you both, and I want things to be right for you when I go. I am giving you a long lease of the Windsor. I had thought about a five-year lease, but you might find the University people hard to deal with when they take over, so I've decided to make it ten. Now - that should set you up.'

I blurted out my gratitude, fighting back tears.

Having made her decision, Mary lost no time in contacting Ken Hatfield. She made a new will, leaving relatively small amounts to Mrs Boom and her senior staff. Bequests of around the same value were left to her sisters, Lolly and Toby, and to three of Daisy's granddaughters. With these few exceptions the new will excluded her family. The estrangement of some family members, dating back to the time of her marriage to Joe and subsequent efforts by them to oust Mary from control of her own companies, had caused wounds that were never healed.

In discussions prior to formalising arrangements to leave the bulk of her estate to the University, Mary spoke forcefully about her expectations regarding the administration of the legacy.

'I want my money to be used to find a cure for the illness that took Joe from me. I grieve every day because I couldn't find a doctor to do something for him, and I can't help thinking of all those other women who lose their husbands in the same way. It's a tragedy.

'I want all the money earned by the estate to go into medical research. I don't want any of the funds spent on buildings or monuments in honour of Joe or myself. In my opinion there are probably enough of those already, and the money could be better spent.'

The Deed of Trust, executed by Mary Bertha Raine and The University of Western Australia, was signed on 8 August 1957. In essence, it set out the format for management of Mary's properties when the University became owners after her death. It also formalised the agreement, already in place, whereby Mary's interest in Joe's estate was gifted by her to the University.

Key points from the document are quoted here.

> The University shall with the capital of the Fund establish a perpetual fund to be known as 'THE ARNOLD YELDHAM AND MARY RAINE MEDICAL RESEARCH FOUNDATION' (hereinafter called 'the Foundation') and the University shall invest the Fund and be possessed thereof as hereinafter mentioned.
> The net income of the Fund subject to Clause 8 (c) hereof shall be applied by the University in and towards the seeking diagnosing and investigating the nature origin and cause of disease in human beings with initial emphasis on arterio sclerosis and allied diseases and the prevention cure alleviation and combating of such diseases.

Mary's confidence in the existing, and potential value of the real estate she had acquired was such that her desire to keep her properties intact was expressed in the Deed, but in such a way as to allow the University freedom to act at all times in its own best interests.

> The Donor hereby FURTHER DECLARES AND IT IS HEREBY MUTUALLY AGREED AND DECLARED that the University may :
> At any time and from time to time sell any real or personal property forming part of the Fund for such sum and upon such

terms and conditions as the University may in its absolute and unfettered discretion think fit but it is the wish of the Donor and without in any way creating a Trust or binding obligation and without limiting the unfettered discretion of the University that no real estate shall be sold unless the University considers that such sale is in the best interests of the Foundation .

The Deed of Trust provided that on Mary's death, the University would become owner of the following properties.

Wentworth Hotel - freehold and business
Bohemia Hotel
United Service Hotel - freehold and business
Windsor Hotel
Williams Building
House on Cnr Preston and Mary Streets, Como
House in Melville Parade, South Perth
Number of shops in William Street
Bon Marche Arcade

Mary felt strangely comforted by her decision, and once the formalities were in place she began to enjoy a peace she had not known since the start of Joe's illness. We shared with her the happy news that our second child was due to arrive in late December.

It was some months before reports of Mary Raine's generosity became public. On 26 November 1957 the front page of *The Daily News* carried this report.

Mrs. M.B.Raine, of the Wentworth Hotel made one of the biggest bequests ever to the WA University, said Premier Albert Hawke: This generous action will remain as a very worthwhile example to other citizens.
As one who has been directly associated with the successful moves to establish a medical school in WA, I have been greatly impressed with the generosity of Mrs Raine and her late husband. Their very substantial financial support of the medical school will enable much research work to be undertaken.
Said Vice-Chancellor Stanley Prescott:
Mrs. Raine's bequest will encourage medical research in all its aspects.
The entire State must share in the gratitude we feel towards Mrs. Raine.

Suddenly, Perth 'discovered' Mary Raine. She found herself the focus of the kind of media attention she had taken pains to avoid all her life.

Relatives with whom she had little, or no contact, since her marriage to Joe, started to get in touch. 'Begging' letters arrived in embarrassing numbers, some of them hand-delivered, a fact which Mary found very distressing and difficult to deal with. She was often approached when working on the lounge desk, and there was no escape from the hard luck stories that preceded requests for money.

Mary was reputed to be tough, even hard, when it came to giving, but surprisingly, she could be caught off her guard. One woman who arrived with a small boy in tow, told such a tale of privation, hardship and misery, that she completely shattered Mary's defences. The woman may have been in genuine need, or just a clever actress. Either way, she left with the promise of weekly assistance, and collected regularly until Mary's death.

Our second son, Joel Edward Sangster was born on 31 December 1957. Mary, with Mrs Boom , Hilda and Les came to the Windsor to see the new baby in mid-January. We were sitting under the trees in the garden, with Shadow, our Collie dog, beside the pram. I mentioned that Shadow was in disgrace. He had always been so gentle but earlier in the week had behaved entirely out of character, when he chased the postman's bike and bit the poor man on the ankle, tearing his trousers into the bargain. Mary followed the story intently.

'You know why the dog behaved like that? He's jealous of the new baby, and I'd advise you not to leave him alone with Joel. Collies are known to become sour as they get older, and you'll have to be very careful. Now, I hope you're taking notice of me.'

I did take notice, and we gave Shadow to a country visitor who had always made a great fuss of the dog.

In the years following Joe's death, Mary's health gradually deteriorated. It was as if she no longer had the strength or the will to fight health problems she had previously kept at bay by sheer determination and a stubborn refusal to accept that they existed at all. She was used to bouts of pneumonia, and had become aware there was a bowel problem, but had chosen to ignore it. Now, she was warned, she could no longer do that. There were intermittent visits to hospital.

Mary looked forward to the regular letters from her sister, Elsie, and regretted that there was such a vast distance between them. When Elsie wrote asking for help to buy a new home, Mary responded quickly and sent money for the purchase. She only wished she felt well enough to make the trip to see it, but she knew her travelling days were over.

Elsie wrote to Mary on 26 July 1958, from the new home at Mill Hill.

> I understand well how you must miss Joe, he really was a dear. I shall always picture you both at 7 Hillside and (remember) the happy times we all spent together, despite the bouts of sickness you had.
> Appleyards closed their Finchley Road shop - it was the most modern and high class before the war - it had a good family trade, but since, things are very different: most people go to the shops to select their goods. Before, they ordered them. Supermarkets where you can buy everything must be hitting the small traders.
> Charlie and Ivy are both far from well, and I worry about them. I understand Margot (their daughter) has written to you asking for help. I hope you will be able to do something for them dear. Birdie dear, again I do thank you for everything.
> (Signed) Elsie [6]

As the months passed Mary became less able to play an active role in the running of the hotel. The University had installed its accountant, Roland Fletcher, to oversee the management of the Wentworth and Mary's other properties. She was relieved to surrender the burden of responsibility.

When Mary visited the Windsor some time in May 1959, I told her there would be an addition to our family early in the following January.

'How lovely dear. A girl this time. You are going to be kept busy, but I'm sure you know that. I hope it all goes well for you. I used to think it would be impossible to have small children around a hotel, but you seem to have managed without too much trouble.'

It was the last time Mary was well enough to come to see us. In November, she became ill and was admitted for surgery to St John of God Hospital in Subiaco. Elsie sent a brief note dated 15 December 1959.

> This is just a short letter to say how very sorry dear we were to hear that you have had to undergo another operation and do most sincerely hope that you are now making progress and will get well again as soon as you can, with your indomitable willpower, you will dear.
> (Signed) Elsie [7]

I visited Mary regularly whilst she was in hospital and had to face the sad truth that she was unlikely to recover sufficiently to pick up the threads of her life. When she did return to the Wentworth, round-the-clock nurses were engaged to care for her, but the following weeks saw Mary in and out of hospital with sad regularity. She was strong enough to spend Christmas in the surroundings she loved, but early in the New Year was admitted to Royal Perth Hospital. I visited her there to tell her she had predicted correctly. Our daughter, Julienne, was born on 17 January 1960.

Mary died on 3 February 1960, just two weeks before her 83rd birthday. On 5 February, she was laid to rest beside her beloved Rainee.

Unlike Joe's funeral, which was very well-attended, Mary's final journey was a quiet affair. A few family members, some friends, staff, and representatives from the University, made up the number of mourners. As I wept at the rear of the silent gathering, I couldn't help thinking it was hardly a fitting finale to what had been such an outstanding performance.

A tribute in the words of Dr Carl Georgeff, her physician and close friend of long standing, captures the essence of Mary Raine.

> No single paragraph could hope to define the complex character of Mary Raine. Brought up in the mid-Victorian era of female recessiveness, by dint of perseverance and sheer force of character, she was able to succeed in a male-dominated world. This undoubtedly made her appear hard and even harsh, in her business dealings. To her husband and her family she gave lavishly both in affection and worldly goods.
>
> Throughout her life, Mary Raine showed great business acumen. In the establishment of the Raine Research Foundation, she saw what she called 'a good business deal'. Her fortune could be used by generations of medical researchers to try to answer the problems that remained unanswered during her own life time.
>
> It is hoped that this last business venture of Mary Raine will be a triumph, and a monument to a woman who became a benefactress of mankind.

The following tribute was published in The Hotel Review on 29 February 1960.

OBITUARY

A long association with hotelkeeping in this State was ended with the passing on 3rd February of Mrs Mary Bertha Raine, after an illness of four months.

The late Mrs Raine, formerly Mrs Thomas, had extensive property interests including the Wentworth, United Service and Bohemia Hotels, Perth, and the Windsor Hotel, South Perth.

Her husband, Arnold Yeldham Raine, predeceased her in February , 1957.

Much of her estate will be directed to the University Medical School in the form of a trust to be known as the Arnold Yeldham and Mary Raine Medical Research Foundation. A splendid gesture for which she will be remembered and honoured.

The Raine Family Crest

Faith Dispels Fear

Chapter 13

THE RAINE FOUNDATION: A unique achievement

The following Report is provided by Lyn Ellis, Executive Officer of the Raine Foundation

BACKGROUND

The Raine Medical Research Foundation represents the largest recent bequest left to The University of Western Australia. It is the leading provider of non-government funds for medical research in WA, second only to the National Health and Medical Research Council (NHMRC). Established by Mary Raine through her legacy to the University, the value of the Raine portfolio has grown from £1m in 1957 to $24m by the year 2002, with total contributions to medical research exceeding $19m.

Over the years, the Raine Foundation has made a distinguished contribution to medical research: it has supported scores of major research projects, funded two Centres of Excellence, established fellowships and scholarships, sponsored the visits of international scholars, participated in major joint ventures and fostered medical research at the undergraduate level.

The foundation is administered by a Research Commitee appointed by the University Senate in accordance with the Deed of Trust, the main objective being to fund investigative research into human disease. Mary Raine was quite explicit in her wishes as documented at Clause 3(b) of the Deed, which states that:

> *the net income of the Fund shall be applied towards seeking, diagnosing and investigating the nature, origin and causes of diseases in human beings, with*

the initial emphasis on arteriosclerosis and allied diseases, and the prevention, cure, alleviation and combating of such diseases.

It was also Mary Raine's express wish that her long-time friend and personal physician, Dr Carl Georgeff, fulfil a major role in the administration of the Foundation. She appointed Dr Georgeff a member of the Research Committee in perpetuity, or until he chose to resign, and he was the guiding hand behind the Raine Foundation for more than thirty years. During this time Dr Georgeff's single-minded commitment and special understanding of Mary Raine's wishes, saw the Foundation develop into a major funding body with annual allocations exceeding $1.2m.

Financial Management

At the time of making her bequest, Mary Raine appointed the University as Financial Manager of her properties and investments, with her estate eventually to be used for the purpose of establishing the Raine Medical Research Foundation in perpetuity, and the income distributed each year for the benefit of medical research.

The most significant change to the Raine portfolio took place in 1998 with the sale of the two remaining properties purchased by Mary Raine - the Hotel Windsor and Raine Square, which included the Wentworth Hotel. The decision to sell was the culmination of an extensive feasibility study of Perth property values by the University Fund Manager, along with a review of the Raine investment portfolio and funding objectives. It was also in line with the University decision at the time to diversify its large property portfolio, which previously had been tightly focused in Western Australia. This decision was taken to ensure that Raine would hold a balanced portfolio with better long-term financial yields, and a Capital Fund that would keep pace with inflation and continue to grow. The Raine investment portfolio has been carefully structured to protect the capital base of the Foundation whilst adhering to the Raine charter to support the needs and aspirations of future generations of medical researchers.

Early Research Initiatives

Looking back to the early 1960s, it is clear that the Raine Foundation played a crucial role in supporting research at that time. The Medical School was in its infancy and while the importance of scientific research was acknowledged, problems associated with the geographical separation of departments and financial stringencies restricted the pace of development and scope for training.

Although funding was very limited, Raine was able to make a significant impact. It sponsored a number of important projects, including the Raine Medical Statistics Unit and the well-known Busselton Population Study, and introduced a Student Exchange Scheme and Visiting Professorships Scheme.

Raine also provided substantial funding to The National Heart Foundation of Australia. Between 1973 and 1980, along with several other research granting organisations, Raine supported a therapeutic trial of anti-hypertensive drugs in subjects with mild symptomless hypertension. *The Blood Pressure Study* was to become one of the major achievements of cardiovascular medicine in Australia and, in the words of the 2001 National Heart Foundation Director of Health, Medical and Scientific Affairs, 'it put Australia on the world map.' In August 2001 Professor Andrew Tonkin advised the Raine Foundation that 'until studies such as this had established the value of treating young hypertensives, this now universally-accepted evidence was questioned. The consequent impact of the Study on stroke, coronary heart disease and cardiac failure, and the personal toll they exact, has been immense.' In his chapter entitled: *The Australian National Blood Pressure Study 1973 - 1979,* Professor Ralph Reader, Medical Director and Chief Executive of the National Heart Foundation at that time paid tribute to the Raine Medical Research Foundation for meeting all costs for the Perth centre for this Study.

Centres of Excellence

In 1980 the Foundation turned its attention to more long-term projects with the establishment of two Centres of Excellence. Mary Raine had requested that the initial emphasis of medical research be directed towards investigating cardiovascular disease, and the Committee wanted to ensure that her wishes were fulfilled. One of the Raine Centres of Excellence was devoted to studies involving atherosclerosis and vascular disease. The Centres were:

The Epidemiology, Aetiology and Community Control of Hypertensive and Atherosclerotic Vascular Disease
Department of Medicine

Perinatal and Developmental Biology
Department of Physiology

Raine continued to sponsor the two Centres of Excellence for the following eight years, from 1980 to 1988, while continuing its support for the Busselton Population Study and the Medical Statistics Unit.

Introduction of Major Research Grants

Project Funding

In 1989 after a review of Raine funding allocations, under the guidance of Dr Georgeff, it was agreed that the initial commitment to cardiovascular research had been fulfilled. It was time to broaden the areas of research supported by the Foundation to include the wider scientific community. As a result, Major Grants were established and in due course these became the prime focus of annual funding. These were designed to provide greater flexibility and to give more researchers the opportunity to apply for Raine funding.

It is particularly noteworthy that the most ambitious project to be supported by the Raine Foundation was in response to a grant application from Professor John Newnham in 1989. A grant of $640,000 was approved The project was initially entitled: *The origins of disease in the fetus, the child and the young adult: A Western Australian Pregnancy Cohort Study.* This was later renamed *The Raine Study.* Professor Newnham's project was based on the hypothesis that adult diseases had their origins before birth. With colleagues, Professor Con Michael, Professor Lou Landau and Professor Fiona Stanley, Professor Newnham embarked on what has become, the world's largest study of this type.

It has been proven that susceptibility to blood pressure, hypertension, heart disease and stroke are largely determined by prenatal factors.

It is significant that twelve years after the *Raine Study* was funded in 1989, Professor Newnham was invited to present his work at the first International Congress on *Foetal Origins of Adult Disease*, held in Bombay, India in April 2001. Professor Newnham is most proud that a grant made possible by Mary Raine's generosity, supported a study of such importance. It is also noteworthy that this study investigates the origin of the disease that claimed the life of her beloved husband, Joe. It was Mary's earnest wish that this disease should be investigated and better understood and, if possible a cure found, for the benefit of future generations.

Medical Research Initiatives

Nineteen ninety-six proved to be a significant year for the Raine Foundation. For the first time, funding exceeded $2m, with twelve major grants worth a total of $1.5m being allocated, and the introduction of Distinguished Visitors' Awards. Raine also entered into co-operative joint ventures with two other major WA organisations, the State Government Insurance Office and the Cancer Foundation of Western Australia Inc. to establish two new joint awards:

> *The Raine/SGIO Postgraduate Scholarship; and*
>
> *The Raine/Cancer Foundations' Fellowship and Research Award*

The SGIO acknowledged the importance of medical research in generously agreeing to support the introduction of two postgraduate Scholarships on a shared-funding basis. These Scholarships were very important because they were offered during a period of economic constraint, and provided financial support for young graduates at a critical time in their research career. The Scholarships continued to be awarded for the following three years.

Raine was also pleased to announce a three-year joint initiative with the Cancer Foundation, matching a contribution of $150,000 to fund research into the causes and treatment of cancer. In December 1996 Dr Deirdre Coombe was awarded the Fellowship for her project entitled: *The role of the melanoma associated antigen, MUC18, in metastatic melanoma.*

In 1999, Raine formed a partnership with the Keogh Institute for Medical Research, in establishing a $300,000 research initiative into reproductive medicine. This three-year Keogh/Raine Memorial Fellowship, a tribute to the late Professor E J (Ted) Keogh for his research into Reproductive Medicine, was awarded to Dr Karin Eidne for her project entitled: *G-protein coupled receptors and signalling components of the reproductive system.*

The year 2000 was also another important milestone in the history of the Raine Medical Research Foundation. Forty years had passed since the Foundation was established and it was time to reflect on past achievements, to review the processes that had been put in place, and to look to new opportunities for the future.

The Research Committee was keen to ensure that scientific excellence remained the underlying principle for the award of Raine Grants, bearing in mind that financial accountability was fundamental to the development of sound policies and long-term strategies. With these aims in mind, a review was commissioned to assess project grants awarded over the ten-year period, 1989-1998. The review was completed in September 2000 and a comprehensive report produced that outlined a range of important issues. The results of the Raine Review would assist the Committee to evaluate past decisions and trends and to consider new directions for the future. It was particularly pleasing to note that eighty-five percent of research scientists who received a Raine Grant, went on to achieve success with other major funding bodies.

It is clear that the Raine Foundation has made a major impact on medical research in Western Australia through the projects it has supported and the initiatives it has introduced. Forty years after Mary Raine's passing, the Foundation is in a sound financial position. It holds a balanced and diversified portfolio that promises long-term financial yields, and it has a record of outstanding achievement in its support for medical research. It is administered by a group of professional scholars, led by the Deputy Vice-Chancellor, who are committed to the philosophy of the Raine Foundation.

The Raine Foundation certainly holds a unique place in the advancement of learning in Western Australia and while the University was the recipient of this major philanthropic bequest, it is the general community who are the real beneficiaries of Mary Raine's incredible generosity.

Summary

The Raine Foundation provided in excess of $19m for medical research in Western Australia between 1960 and 2002. These funds supported a range of medical research projects and initiatives as listed below:

The Raine Medical Statistics Unit (1965-1984)

The Busselton Population Studies (1969-1975, 1979)

Visiting Professorships (1971 - ongoing)
The Raine Visiting Professors' Scheme (est.1971)
Raine Distinguished Visitors' Awards (est. 1996)

Centres of Excellence (1980-1988):
The Raine Centre for the Study of Epidemiology, Aetiology and Community Control of Hypertensive and Atherosclerotic Vascular Disease
The Raine Centre for the Study of Perinatal and Developmental Biology

Major Research Grants (1989-1996)
45 Major Research Grants

Raine Small Grants (1994)
6 Pilot Small Research Grants

Raine Priming Grants (1997-2002, ongoing)
43 Priming Grants

Joint Fellowships and Research Awards (1997-2001)

The Raine/Cancer Foundations' Fellowship and Research Award (1997-1999)

The Keogh/Raine Fellowship and Research Award (1999-2001)

Scholarships

Vacation Scholarships (1967-1985)

Overseas Travelling Scholarships (1972-1975)

Raine/SGIO Postgraduate Scholarships (1996-1998)

Raine Bachelor of Medical Science Scholarships (1992 - ongoing)

Major Sponsorships

Australian Society for Medical Research, WA Medical Research Week (1996 - ongoing)

Lotteries Commission Medical Research Symposium (1998)

Research Project

The Urological Research Centre Project (1995-1998)

The Raine Foundation also funded other medical research initiatives over the years. Among these were a Student Exchange Programme, a Postdoctoral Fellowship, a Research Fellow, as well as a grant to the Postgraduate Education Committee.

INTERVIEWS CONDUCTED BY THE AUTHOR and WRITTEN SUBMISSIONS

Ethel Allen (nee Boom)	Daughter of Mary Raine's receptionist
Paddy Baker	Permanent guest at Wentworth Hotel
Nell Bowles	Staff member at Wentworth Hotel
Len Brennan	Staff member The West Australian
Hilda Brown (nee Boom)	Daughter of Mary Raine's receptionist
Mary Coward	Mary Raine's niece
Rose (Roz) Dearing (nee Boom)	Daughter of Mary Raine's receptionist
John Friend	Father farmed at Manmanning with Joe Raine
Zoe Garbutt	Granddaughter of Abraham Krakouer
Pat Garland	Remembered Mary Raine's brush with a robber
Dr Carl Georgeff	Mary Raine's physician and personal friend
Robert F Goodhart	US Submariner in Perth during war years
Beryl Hobson	Mary Raine's niece
Ivy Hogan	Staff member at the Gordons and Wentworth Hotels
Fred Jones	Farmer from Manmanning
Harry Love	Apprentice to Mary Raine's hairdresser
Harry Murray	Apprenticed to business next Bohemia Hotel
Professor John Newnham	Joint recipient of significant Raine grant
Guy Palmer	Harvey resident interested in local history
Kathleen Pouleris	War bride of American submariner

Ailsa Raymond	Granddaughter of Mary Raine's sister
Barney Richards	Mary Raine's accountant
Glenys Rosling	Granddaughter of Mary Raine's brother
Francis (Gunner) Signori	US Submariner in Perth during war years
Morgan Smith	Father knew Mary Raine in Mornington Mills
Martie Sundstrum	Private nurse to Mary Raine
Terri-ann White	Great-niece of Abraham Krakouer
Elizabeth Williams	Great-granddaughter of Abraham Krakouer
Ruth Williams	Apprenticed to Mary Raine's dressmaker

ARCHIVAL and GENERAL SOURCES of REFERENCE

Alexander Library, Perth
Battye Library, Perth
Broome Historical Society: Val Burton
Defence Department Archives
Department of Land Management
Bruce Duckham, Floreat
Floreat Library
Lou Fryer: Archival Taped History of Harvey
Guildford Grammar School Archives: Rosemary Waller
Basil Hand: Retired Estate Officer, Raine Foundation
Nyngan Historical Society: Nancy Brooksby
Raine Foundation: Lyn Ellis, Executive Officer
State Archives, Perth
Supreme Court Archives
University of Western Australia Archives

REFERENCE ORIGINS - BOOKS, ARTICLES and REPORTS

Seaman, L.C.B. *Life In Victorian London*, (Norwich, UK: Fletcher & Son Ltd, 1973).

The Queen's London, (London: Cassell & Company, Limited).

Farwell, Byron. *The Great Boer War*, (USA: Harper & Rowe, 1976).

Hibbert, Christopher. *Queen Victoria in her Letters and Journals,* (London: John Murray, 1984).

Weintraub, Stanley. *Biography of a Queen*, (London: Unwin Hyman, 1987).

Flink, James J. *The Automobile Age*, (USA: Massachusetts Institute of Technology, 1988).

Lofts, Nora. *Domestic Life In England*, (London: George Weidenfeld & Nicholson Ltd, 1976).

Johnson, Louise. *Gaslight Sydney - The city viewed through late Victorian eyes.* (Sydney: Allen and Unwin, 1984).

Kennedy, Buzz. *Sydney's Own - 25 years of the Sheraton Wentworth,* (Sydney: Focus Books Pty Ltd).

Appleyard, R.T. *Australia and immigration*, (Canberra: Australian National University, 1964).

Lawson, Ronald. *Brisbane in the 1890s: A Study of an Australian urban society,* (Queensland: University of Queensland Press, 1973).

Members of Nyngan Historical Society. *Nyngan on the Bogan 1883-1983,* (Dubbo NSW: Macquarie Publications, 1983).

Austen, Tom. *The Streets of Old Perth*, (Perth: St George Books, 1988).

Mossenson, David. *Hebrew, Israelite, Jew: History of the Jews of Western Australia*, (Nedlands WA: University of Western Australia Press, 1990).

Bolton, G.C. *A Fine Country To Starve In,* (Nedlands WA: University of Western Australia Press, 1972).

Crowley, Frank. *A Documentary History of Australia -4- Modern Australia*, (Melbourne: Wren Publishing, 1973).

Tuckfield, T.T. *Early Days - Journal of The Western Australian Historical Society, Vol 7 Part 3*, (Perth: Western Australian Historical Society, 1977).

Salmon, H.E. *Perth in the Depression Years*, (Perth: Suburban News of the West Australian).

Commonwealth Department of Works, Perth Branch. *History of the United Service Hotel*, (Report prepared by the Architectural Division, 1968).

Welborn, Suzanne. *The History of a Brewery,* (Nedlands WA: University of Western Australia Press, 1987).

Ed. Wright, Ernest Hunter, and Mary Hermitage. *Richards Topical Encyclopaedia - Vol 6*, (Canada: The Richards Company, Inc, 1962).

Commonwealth Department of Works, Perth Branch. *The Statewide Survey of Hotels,* (Perth; 1968).

Bain, Mary Albertus. *Full Fathom Five*, (Perth: Artlook Books, 1982).

Edwards, Hugh. *Port of Pearls*, (Sydney: Rigby Publications, 1983).

The West Australian Licensed Victuallers' Gazette, Perth.

The West Australian Newspaper, Perth.

The Daily News, Perth.

Barker, Anthony J. and Jackson, *Lisa. Fleeting Attraction*, (Nedlands WA: University of Western Australia Press, 1996).

Cairns, Lynne. *Fremantle's Secret Fleets*, (Fremantle, WA: Western Australian Maritime Bureau, 1995).

Gregory, Jenny, ed. *On The Homefront - Western Australia and World War II*, (Nedlands, WA: University of Western Australia Press, 1996).

Beaumont, Joan, ed. *Australia's War, 1939-1945*, (Sydney: Allen and Unwin Ltd, 1996).

Members of Bullsbrook Historical Society. *Memories of Chittering and Bullsbrook*, (Perth: Access Press, 1996).

NOTES

Chapter 1 *Here's one you won't have to keep*

1 Interview: Mary Coward.
2 Ibid.
3 Ibid.
4 Oral history: Mary Raine.
5 Ibid.
6 Journal: Mary Raine.
7 Interview: Mary Coward.
8 Interview: Ailsa Raymond.
9 Journal: Mary Raine.
10 Interview: Ailsa Raymond.
11 Journal: Mary Raine.
12-19 Ibid.
20 Letter of reference: Mary Raine's employer.
21 Journal: Mary Raine.
22-27 Ibid.
28 Interview: Mary Coward.
29 Interview: Ailsa Raymond.
30 Journal: Mary Raine.
31 Hibbert: Queen Victoria in her Letters and Journals,p.335.
32 Journal: Mary Raine.
33 Oral History: Mary Raine.
34 Ibid.
35 Journal: Mary Raine.
36 Ibid.
37 Interview: Mary Coward and Beryl Hobson.
38 Oral history: Mary Raine.
39 Interview: Mary Coward and Beryl Hobson.

Chapter 2 *We have come to God's own country*

1 Oral history: Mary Raine.
2-5 Ibid.
6 Interview: Ailsa Raymond.
7 Oral history: Mary Raine.
8-11 Ibid.

Chapter 3 *Always be in debt: It is the only way to make money*

1 Oral history: Mary Raine.
2-4 Ibid.
5 Interview: Ailsa Raymond.
6-7 Ibid.
8 Oral history: Mary Raine.
9-11 Ibid.
12 Interview: Mary Coward.
13 Interview: Ailsa Raymond.
14 Interview: Morgan Smith.
15 Oral history: Mary Raine.
16 Interview: Guy Palmer.
17 Oral History: Lou Fryer.
18 Oral history: Mary Raine.
19 Ibid.
20 Interview: Glenys Rosling.
21 Ibid.
22 Oral history: Mary Raine.
23-24 Ibid.
25 Interview: Terri-ann White.
26 Interview: Zoe Garbutt.
27 Interview: Elizabeth Williams.
28-29 Ibid.
30 Interview: Ailsa Raymond.
31 Interview: Zoe Garbutt.
32-33 Ibid.
34 Interviews: Terri-ann White, Zoe Garbutt, Ailsa Raymond.
35 Oral history: Mary Raine.
36-38 Ibid.

Chapter 4 *Speculate to accumulate*

1 Interview: Mary Coward.
2 Oral history: Mary Raine.
3-4 Ibid.
5 The West Australian, 13 April 1928, p.8.
6 The West Australian, 15 May 1928, p.9.
7 Oral history: Mary Raine.
8-11 Ibid.

12 Oral history: Joe Raine.
13 Oral history: Mary Raine.
14 Interview: Pat Garland.
15 United Licensed Victuallers' Gazette (ULVG): September 1928.
16 ULVG, December 1936.
17 Oral history: Mary Raine.
18 Interview: Hilda Brown.
19 Interview: Mary Coward.
20 Interview: Ruth Williams.
21 Interview: Hilda Brown.
22 Interview: Harry Love.
23 Interview: Len Brennan.

Chapter 5 *It is my melancholy duty*

1 Oral history: Mary Raine.
2 Interview: Zoe Garbutt.
3 Oral history: Mary Raine.
4 Interview: Roz Dearing.
5 Oral history: Mary Raine.
6 Barker and Jackson: Fleeting Attraction, p.200.
7 Interview: Kathleen Pouleris.
8 Ibid.
9 Oral history: Mary Raine.
10 Interview: Roz Dearing.
11 State Licensing Court Records.
12 Correspondence: Frank (Gunner) Signori.
13 Ibid.
14 Correspondence: Robert F Goodhart.
15 Interview: Len Brennan.
16 Dr Carl Georgeff.
17 Interview: Harry Murray.
18 Interview: Morgan Smith.
19 Barker and Jackson: Fleeting Attraction. p.192.
20 Interview: Roz Dearing.
21 Welborn: The History of a Brewery, p.172.
22 Barker and Jackson: Fleeting Attraction. p.194.
23 Ibid: p.195, p.196.

24 Interview: Roz Dearing.
25 Oral history: Mary Raine.
26 State Licensing Court Records.

Chapter 6 *Rainee*

1 Timewell: Uninews - Strong Foundations, 5 August 1991,p.1.
2 Church Records: St John's Wesleyan Church, Fremantle.
3 Timewell: Uninews - Strong Foundations, 5 August 1991,p.1.
4 Oral history: Joe Raine.
5 School archives: Guildford Grammar School.
6 Archives: Broome Historical Society.
7 Article: Nor West Echo, 25 July 1925, p.12.
8 Oral history; Joe Raine.
9 Interview: Fred Jones.
10 Interview: John Friend.
11-12 Ibid.
13 Interview: Andrea Bear.
14 Interview: Fred Jones.
15 Ibid.
16 Oral history: Joe Raine.
17 Oral history: Pat (Paddy) Baker.
18-20 Ibid.
21 Oral history: Joe Raine.

Chapter 7 *We were two pals*

1 Oral history: Mary Raine.
2 Ibid.
3 Oral history: Paddy Baker.
4 Interview: Fred Jones.
5 Interview: Mary Coward.
6 Oral history: Mary Raine.
7 Interview: Beryl Hobson.
8 Interview: Ailsa Raymond.
9-10 Ibid.
11 Interview: Nell Bowles
12 Interview: Ivy Hogan.

13 Oral history: Joe Raine.
14 Interview: Barney Richards.

Chapter 8 *It's the best room in the hotel*
1 Written memoir: Mary Coward.

Chapter 9 *We hope you'll say 'Yes'*

Chapter 10 *We want to retire*
1 Written memoir: Beryl Hobson.
2 Oral history: Mary Raine.
3 Correspondence: Charles Carter to Mary raine.
4 Correspondence: Elsie Norchi to Mary Raine.
5 Written Memoir: Laura (Lolly) Cooke.
6 Written Memoir: Beryl Hobson.

Chapter 11 *So dearly loved: So sadly missed*
1 Interview: Martie Sundstrum.
2 Interview: Ethel Allen.

Chapter 12 *The long day closes*
1 Interview: Hilda Brown.
2-3 Ibid.
4 Oral history: Paddy Baker.
5 Ibid.
6 Correspondence: Elsie Norchi to Mary Raine.
7 Ibid.

PICTURE CREDITS

Author's Collection: 61, 145, 163
Broome Historical Society: 91
Guildford Grammar School Archives: 87
The Raine Foundation: 13, 101, 103, 107, 185
Ailsa Raymond: 41
The West Australian: cover, 53, 55, 175

INDEX

Abbott, Valentine, 49, 110, 176, 177
Adelphi Theatre, 14
Ainsworth (nee Carter), Millicent, 31, 35, 49, 110, 111, 113, 117
Alambra Bars, 38
Allen (nee Boom), Ethyl, 94, 165
Allen, Harry, 165

Baker, Paddy, 73, 95, 96, 100, 136, 173, 176
Barker, Anthony, 74, 79, 80
Barker, Bill, 74
Blackman, Charlie, 88, 90, 91
Bohemia Hotel, 38, 54, 56, 57, 66, 67, 80, 179
Bon Marche Arcade, 131, 179
Bon Ton Cafe, 39, 40, 42-44, 46
Boom, Louisa, 64-66, 73, 80, 100, 125, 126, 132, 149, 150, 172, 173, 177, 180
Bowles, Nell, 118
Brennan, Len, 66, 78
Brooksby, Nancy, 25
Brown (nee Boom), Hilda, 65, 172, 173, 180
Brown, Les, 172, 173, 180
Bullsbrook Hotek, 67, 68, 69, 70
Burton, Val, 88, 91

Cafe Anglais, 46
Cafe de Paris, 54
Carter, Charles, 2, 5, 7-9, 11, 12, 18
Carter, Charles (Charlie), 153, 181
Carter (m. Carter), Daisy, 1, 3, 5, 18, 21-27, 29-32, 128, 177
Carter, Dora, 46, 62
Carter (m. Norchi), Elsie, 105, 153, 154, 181, 182
Carter (m. Reinke), Florence (Toby), 46, 62, 100, 158, 177
Carter, Frederick Ernest, 31, 110-114
Carter, Frederick John, 31
Carter, George, 38, 49, 50, 56, 57, 60, 69, 70, 105, 112, 116
Carter, Gertrude, 46
Carter, Ivy, 153, 181
Carter, John (Jack), 46, 62, 116
Carter (m. Cooke), Laura (Lolly), 105, 128, 153-155, 177
Carter, Nellie, 50
Carter, Sydney Frederick (Fred), 38, 49, 50, 110-116
Central Hotel, 31, 33
Chequers Hotel, 69, 70
Coward, Dick, 128, 129
Coward, Mary, 49, 128, 129

Dearing (nee Boom), Roz, 73, 79, 82, 94
Depression, 50, 52, 56-59, 62, 70
Drury Lane, 12, 14
Durack, John, 110, 112-114, 116

Evans, Rod, 76

Fletcher, Roland, 181
Friend, John, 92, 93
Fryer, Lou, 37
Fullagar, John, 116

Garbutt, Zoe, 42, 43, 69
Garland, Pat, 62
Georgeff, Dr Carl, 78, 183, 188
George Hotel, 120
Gladstone, Belle, 64

Glyde and Sons, 54
Goodhart, Robert, 77
Gordons Hotel, 42, 46, 47, 49, 50
Governor Broome Hotel, 132
Guildford Grammar, 86, 162

Hack, Gordon, 66, 67
Harris, Sir Augustus, 11, 12
Harvey, 34, 36, 37, 38, 117
Harvey Hotel, 37
Hatfield, Ken, 174, 177
Healy, Jack, 67
Hobson, Beryl, 151, 153, 154
Hogan, Ivy, 119

Isgar, Florence, 80, 169

Jackson, Lisa, 74, 79, 80
Jones, Fred, 92, 94, 100
Johnston, Sid, 144

King Edward Hotel, 56, 57
Krakouer, Abraham, 40, 42, 43
Krakouer, Rebecca, 42, 43

Licensing Act/Court, 51, 63, 64, 80, 83, 97, 108, 159
Love, Harry, 66

Maclurcan, Hannah, 51
McWilliam, Claude, 110-113
Manning, James, 85
Marlborough House, 120
Marsh (nee Carter), Irene, 31, 111, 114-117
Mary and Preston Sts., Como, 158, 179
Melville Parade, South Perth, 179
Metropole Hotel, 30, 31
Metropolitan Properties, 49, 54, 60, 105, 117
Mornington Mills, 35, 36, 79
Murray, Harry, 79

National Hotel, 22
National Mutual Company, 47, 50, 51, 54
Newmarket Hotel, 38, 70
Newnham, Professor John, 190, 191
Newton, Bill, 68, 70
Novak, Vaclav (Jacko), 120, 172
Nyngan Hotel, 24-26, 50

Ocean Beach Hotel, 74, 77

Palmer, Guy, 37
Phillips Hotel, 22
Popular Cafe, 39, 40
Pouleris, Bill, 74, 75
Pouleris, Kath, 74

Queen Victoria, 4-7, 14, 15

Raine (nee Manning), Jane, 85, 86
Raine (nee Carter) (m. Thomas), Mary (Birdie), 1-18, 19-27, 29-47, 49-68, 69-83, 94-97, 99-121, 123, 126-135, 137-150, 151-160, 161-170, 171-183
Raine Medical Research Foundation, 174, 177-179
Raine, Joe, 43, 59, 68, 85-97, 99-121, 123, 126-135, 137-150, 151-160, 161-170
Raymond, Ailsa, 35, 42, 43, 117
Red Lion Hotel, 38, 50
Resch's Brewery, 26
Richards, Barney, 120, 121
Rosling, Glenys, 38

Sangster, Colin, 149, 159

Sangster, Eric (Cole), 123-136, 137-150, 155-160, 161-170, 177
Sangster, Joel, 180
Sangster, Julienne, 182
Sangster, Mark, 152, 162, 165, 166
Shepherd, Alan, 66, 67
Signori, Francis (Gunner), 76, 77
Skogland (Raine), Mary, 88
Smith, Morgan, 36, 79
State Implement Works, 49, 50
Strickland, George, 59, 60
Sundstrum, Martie, 164

The Deen, 50
Thomas, Bill, 33-37
Timewell, Eileen, 85
Toy, William, 49

Union Hotel, 50
United Licensed Victuallers' Association, 63, 64, 104, 144
United Service Company Limited, 60, 110-116
United Service Hotel, 55, 59, 60, 64, 69, 70, 80, 110-116, 179
University of Western Australia, 59, 116, 120, 159, 167, 174, 177-179, 181, 182

Waller, Rosemary, 86
Wentworth Hotel, 38, 43, 51-56, 58, 62-64, 68, 70, 73-83, 94, 95, 99-108, 118-136, 146, 148, 152-161, 169-179
White, Pat, 79
White, Terri-Ann, 40, 43
Whitely, William, 16
Windsor Hotel, 60, 62, 80, 108, 135-147, 155, 156, 159, 160, 165-167, 177, 179-181
Williams Building, 62, 179
Williams, Elizabeth, 40
Williams, Ruth, 65